Overcoming Trauma

EMMANUEL ADEWUSI

CCCG Publishing House

Copyright © 2025 Emmanuel Adewusi

All rights reserved. No part of this book may be used or reproduced by any means, graphics, electronic, or mechanical, including photocopying, recording, taping, or by any information storage retrieval system without the author's written permission except in cases of brief quotations embodied in critical articles and reviews.

Scriptures are taken from the New King James Version. Copyright 1979, 1980, 1982 by Thomas Nelson, Inc. Used by permission. All right reserved.

Author: Emmanuel Adewusi

ISBN: 978-1-989099-54-4 (hardcover)

ISBN: 978-1-989099-55-1 (e-book)

First Printing 2025

Contents

Dedication	IV
Preface	V
Introduction	1
1. Anatomy of Trauma	5
2. Signs and Symptoms of Trauma	13
3. Traumatized by Your Cross	27
4. Trauma From Within the Church	42
5. The Journey of Deliverance	52
6. Deliverance From Trauma	56
7. Victory in the Mind	71
8. How To Help the Traumatized	80
Epilogue	89
Contact the Author	92
A Sinner's Prayer	93
About the Author	94

Dedication

This book is for the person who senses deep down that something isn't quite right, but hasn't had the language to name it.

You've kept going. You've shown up for others. You've worked hard, served faithfully, and mastered the art of smiling through the pain. But if you're honest, there are places in you that have never fully healed.

You don't need another pep talk. You need true healing and lasting restoration. Not another mask to survive the day, but a mirror to finally see what's broken and begin the journey of becoming whole.

Because no matter how beautiful the building, if the foundation is cracked, it's only a matter of time before everything starts to fall apart. This is your invitation to rebuild from the inside out—to heal, to become whole, and to live from a place of truth.

Preface

Over the years, I have seen what trauma can do when it is ignored or dismissed. I have witnessed people build successful careers, raise families, and even lead ministries—while silently bleeding from wounds they never addressed. I have seen grown men freeze in moments that required strength. I have watched women with so much potential shrink back because of the pain they were taught to hide. And what's most troubling is that many of them didn't even realize trauma was the root.

They just knew something wasn't right. They found themselves easily angered, guarded, emotionally numb, or constantly overthinking. They sabotaged healthy relationships. They pushed people away, expecting rejection before it ever came. And rather than confront the wound, they gave it spiritual language. They called it "discernment" when it was fear. They called it "standards" when it was self-protection.

The truth is, you can be Spirit-filled and still emotionally broken. You can preach the truth and still live in bondage. You can worship with lifted hands and yet have a soul shut down.

Because trauma remains hidden until it is confronted. It buries itself under personality traits, theological vocabulary, and performance, while keeping you functional but fractured.

That is why this book exists. This is your personal invitation to rebuild from the inside out—to heal, to become whole, and to live from a place of truth.

This is not just for people who are "obviously broken." It is for the high-functioning individual who knows how to keep moving but is tired of being triggered. It's for the adult who still feels the sting of childhood rejection. It's for the believer who loves God but silently struggles to trust people, or even themselves.

This journey of overcoming trauma will not just inspire you. It will confront you. But if you are willing to lean in and be honest with yourself, you will not finish this book the same way you started it.

Most people spend their lives avoiding this work. But if you are ready, it will be one of the most pivotal moments in your healing journey.

Introduction

Trauma is an often silent, yet profoundly impactful force that can shape an individual's life in ways they might not fully comprehend. It seeps into every aspect of one's being—emotional, mental, and even physical—leaving behind scars that are not always visible but are deeply felt. Everyone has faced or will face potentially traumatic situations at some point in their life. Whether it's through personal betrayal, loss, accidents, or even seemingly minor incidents that triggered profound emotional responses, trauma does not discriminate.

The journey of overcoming trauma is not a straightforward path. It requires a deep understanding of its roots, manifestations, and the various ways it can be addressed and healed. This book, *"Overcoming Trauma"*, aims to provide not just an understanding of trauma but also practical steps to move from a place of pain to a place of wholeness and victory.

In my many years in ministry, I've encountered countless individuals plagued by the residual effects of trauma. I've witnessed firsthand how it can disrupt lives, relationships, and even one's purpose. However, I've also seen transformation and how individuals have turned their pain into power, their trials into testimonies. This transformation is possible for you as well, as you journey through these pages.

This book is structured to guide you methodically through the various facets of trauma: understanding what it is, recognizing its signs, and exploring its various sources—from personal betrayals and Church-related wounds to deeper spiritual implications. We will delve into biblical examples of trauma and deliverance, offering insights and encouragement from those who have walked similar paths.

One critical aspect we will cover is the difference between deliverance and freedom. While deliverance is an essential step, attaining lasting freedom requires a continual process of healing and growth. You will learn practical steps for dealing with trauma, allowing the deep wounds to be addressed and healed fully.

We will also focus on the mind which is the engine room for life. Your thoughts significantly influence your healing journey. By renewing your mind, you position yourself for complete victory over the trauma that has held you captive.

For those called to minister to others, understanding how to work productively with the traumatized is crucial. This includes extending love, grace, and practical help to those who are navigating their own paths of healing. Whether in professional settings or within your community, this book will provide you with the insights needed to support and uplift those struggling with trauma.

As you turn each page, my prayer is that you will find the strength, hope, and tools needed to overcome your trauma. Remember, you are not alone on this journey. Countless others have walked this path and emerged stronger, and so will you. May this book be a guiding light, leading you towards a future of restored joy, peace, and purpose.

Welcome to your journey of overcoming trauma. It begins now. **But don't just read this book, act on it.** Healing doesn't come from revelation alone, but from the application of your newfound understanding. It is in following the guidance this book offers that lasting freedom is secured. Therefore, if the book says you should forgive, pause and actually extend forgiveness to those you need to forgive

1
Anatomy of Trauma

Trauma is characterized by its ability to freeze, shake, or damage a person's emotional state, will, or perceptions. A traumatized person is one whose soul has been made vulnerable to manipulation, control and eventual dominion. Trauma is a deeply impactful experience that alters various facets of an individual's life, so proper acknowledgment, and intervention are crucial for healing and restoring normalcy.

Trauma is any event or series of events that can place the person's soul in a state of shock, causing significant emotional, psychological, or physical disturbance. Most hospitals have a trauma unit because there are events that can happen to a person's body, putting their system in a state of trauma. The focus here is on the soul – something that the person can see, an event, or someone that can shake their will or damage their emotions. For example, a woman or man stepping into their home and seeing their spouse being intimate with somebody else, right on their bed. It can put them in a state of shock, almost immobilizing them. Everyone is different because our makeup is different. What can traumatize one person might not traumatize another.

The spirit comes alive when an individual is born again, but the soul remains unchanged. If one refuses to work with God or the people God has sent to help rebuild the soul, troubles may persist despite worshiping and praying in the spirit. Anything that triggers deep pain can shock the soul, reverse progress, and make it seem as if one never gave their life to Christ. To understand this further, it's important to examine the different parts of the soul:

- The **mind** processes information, analyzes things, reviews options, and thinks, but does not make decisions

- The **will** is where decisions are made

- **Emotions** are where feelings are experienced

Everyone has a different balance of these components. Some may have a strong mind but weak will and emotions, while others may have a strong will but weak mind and emotions. Trauma can disrupt this balance and cause issues such as indecisiveness, where the will becomes frozen.

Parents should pay attention to their children, as sudden changes in behaviour may indicate a traumatic experience. A once lively child becoming reclusive or a severe introvert could be a sign that something traumatic has happened, even if they are unable to talk about it directly. A personal experience shared by the daughter of a popular minister of the gospel illustrates the long-lasting impact of trauma. At the age of three, she was in a vehicle accident with her father. When he left the car to check on the other party involved, she cried and screamed, fearing abandonment. This experience led to abandonment issues that persisted into adulthood, contributing to multiple divorces. The father later realized that if he had known the impact of his actions, he would have taken her with him when he stepped out of the car.

RECOGNIZING WHEN A SPIRIT IS INVOLVED

The danger of allowing a broken soul to remain unhealed is that it can lead to demonic oppression and possession. When a person does not work with God to bring freedom to their broken soul, their human spirit becomes compromised and vulnerable to demonic influences. Initially, it may start as an external oppression, but if the soul remains broken and defenseless, demonic spirits can eventually take over the person's soul leading to a demonic possession. When this happens, the Holy Spirit is no longer present, and the person's identity becomes defined by the demons that possess them.

If demons have found their way into a person's spirit, because of their broken soul, they can control and influence that individual's thoughts, emotions, and actions. Their personality changes, and they may become fearful, prideful, angry, envious, deceitful, sexual predators, habitual liars, etc. These individuals are no longer merely weak but have now become wicked. This means that they have gone from being ignorant of the damage they are causing to becoming willing participants who will have to face God's judgement for wrongdoing.

In these cases, deliverance must start from their human spirit. Several years ago, while serving as a youth pastor in another ministry, I attended a conference that focused on deliverance from demonic spirits, which are surprisingly prevalent among youth, particularly those from broken homes. Pain, often resulting from experiences such as bullying, harassment, or molestation, can serve as an entry point for demons. During the conference, a young, petite-looking girl who initially appeared normal began to manifest when we started ministering to people. Despite her small stature, even strong men struggled to hold her down due to the spirit of anger manifesting through physical strength.

We took her to a separate room and rebuked the spirit, but nothing changed until a more experienced minister stepped in. The minister asked the girl if she wanted the spirit to remain in her, and she said yes, explaining that it had comforted and helped her when everyone else had abandoned her. After a heartfelt conversation, the girl agreed to allow the Holy Spirit to minister to her. She verbally renounced the spirit, and then we were able to successfully command the spirit of anger to leave her. Her face transformed, the odour on her dissipated, and everything about her changed. She was delivered.

Here are some ways you can discern if/when demonic spirits have stepped into a person's heart because of trauma:

- Experiencing a black out when triggered, indicating a force shutting down the soul and operating the body without their permission. This is different from intentional meditation, as the blackout is sudden and uncontrolled

- Feeling uncomfortable, targeted, or singled out when the atmosphere is charged by the Word of God, worship, or the presence of an anointed person, and the name of the spirit is called

Attempting to learn principles on how to live righteously without first addressing the demonic influence is like trying to eject a virus from a computer that is connected to the source code and has the power to delete the antivirus software itself. You cannot deliver yourself; you must humble yourself and submit to someone who can guide you through the process of deliverance. After deliverance, you will experience a newfound sense of peace, love, joy, and the freedom to laugh and love without restraint.

However, it's important to note that demonized people can remain in Church for extended periods if the spiritual aspect of their struggle has not been adequately addressed. Remember that deliverance is not what a large part of the Church has made it to be. Deliverance does not have to be a dramatic affair with demons screaming, telling stories or people vomiting, etc. It can happen quietly as a powerful message is preached, and you suddenly realize the truth and become set free (John 8:32). Do not fall into the trap of professional deliverance ministers who constantly tell you that someone is after you and request money to help you. A genuine minister of the gospel does not charge for their deliverance efforts. We received the grace freely from God and we are obligated to operate the grace freely (Matthew 10:8).

When an anointed person speaks against a specific spirit, those bound by that spirit may manifest discomfort, anger, or an urgent desire to leave the premises. This reaction indicates the spirit's presence and its fear of being ejected. It is important to recognize the signs of demonic influence and to seek help from experienced, anointed individuals who can guide you through the deliverance process. Only then can you truly begin to learn and apply the principles of living a life that honours God.

TRAUMATIZED PEOPLE IN SCRIPTURE

There are two examples of traumatized people in Scripture that we can learn from: **Moses and Apostle Paul**. These individuals might seem to get results, but their trauma still caused them to end their ministry journey in an undesirable way.

Moses

First, let's consider Moses. He did not grow up with his parents throughout his life. Although it may appear that God strategically placed him in Egypt, Moses likely grew up wondering why he, a Jew, was there while his people were elsewhere. This is similar to the experience of an adopted child who, regardless of the affluence of their adoptive family, may wonder if their biological parents rejected or gave them up. Moses was traumatized by this separation from his people and family. The ease with which Moses ran away from the place he grew up in for 40 years, without looking back or maintaining connections with friends or family, is a sign of trauma. Moses was constantly serving the Israelites without receiving service from them, which led to frustration and anger.

While Moses was always hearing from God, he struggled to receive from God for himself. Only once, in Exodus 33, did Moses make a personal request to God. He told God, *"If I have found favor in your sight, show me your glory."* At this point in their relationship, Moses didn't fully grasp God's love and favour for him. God responded almost immediately, assuring Moses, *"You have found favour in my sight. I will cause my goodness to pass over you."* Moses had a mindset similar to that of the older brother in the parable of the prodigal son. He had access to many blessings but never fully embraced or enjoyed them but he didn't allow many people to get close to him, including Joshua, his wife, and his children. Moses was merely functioning and going through the motions, unlike Jesus, who was a perfect, balanced human being with a full range of emotions.

Eventually, the consequences of Moses' trauma caught up with him. In Numbers 11, when the people complained again, Moses accused God of hating him for making him bear the burden of delivering the people without adequate help. God responded by instructing Moses to gather 70 elders so that He could put His spirit on them. Moses exhibited the mindset of someone who, having escaped death, feels compelled to pay for their life through suffering, a clear indication that something is amiss. Although Joshua made more mistakes than Moses, he still entered the promised land, while Moses did not. Difficulty in receiving and accepting forgiveness points to an underlying issue that needs to be addressed.

Paul

Similarly, Paul was traumatized and rejected by his own people. Despite being an evangelist who understood the eternal consequences of rejecting Christ, Paul expressed great sorrow and continual grief in his heart in Romans 9:1-2. He even wished that he himself could be accursed from Christ for the sake of his fellow Jews. This is a red flag, signalling deep emotional pain. God repeatedly told Paul not to focus on ministering to the Jews, but Paul always found himself drawn back to them. However, he lacked the necessary grace, making it more difficult for the Jews to accept Christ. Each time they rejected the gospel, Paul responded with anger, declaring that he would turn his attention to the Gentiles. In Acts 28, when the Jewish leaders in Rome rejected the gospel, Paul became angry and berated them out of frustration. This behaviour indicates that something was not right.

Both Moses and Paul expressed a willingness to be cut off from God's favour for the sake of the same kinsmen who rejected them. While this might sound altruistic, it is evidence of how worthless they felt, i.e. they had a sense of unworthiness and feeling undeserving of the good things they experienced. The Bible teaches that the things written in Scripture are for our learning so that we may be perfected. We can learn from both the positive examples and the mistakes made by these biblical figures. Trauma can be deeply buried until something triggers it. Even if someone believes they are perfect and everything is fine, it is crucial to address any underlying issues. By examining the lives of Moses and Paul, we can gain insight into the impact of trauma and the importance of seeking healing and wholeness in our own lives. Through a closer relationship with God and a willingness to confront our pain, we can experience the freedom and abundant life that Christ offers.

2

Signs and Symptoms of Trauma

There are signs that reveal when trauma is present, whether you realize it or not. It does not always come with loud pain or dramatic breakdowns. Sometimes, it shows up subtly: in how you respond to love, how you handle correction, or how you protect yourself even when no one is attacking you. While self-awareness is not the full solution, it is a necessary starting point. If you don't know what to look for, you'll mislabel survival behaviours as personality traits and call dysfunction your norm.

Even after healing from past wounds, life will continue to present moments that can traumatize you. That's why it's important to be equipped. When you understand the signs, you'll be able to discern what's really going on and invite God into the process before the trauma takes deeper root.

Let's look at some of the common signs and symptoms of trauma.

Gratitude is Difficult

Gratitude is a key indicator of a healthy soul. When God cleanses us thoroughly and completely we begin to see life differently. You realize that every time you wake up, you have many reasons to be grateful. Each day may come with its challenges, but those challenges are no longer enough to weigh us down. They may press, but they don't crush.

However, when you've been carrying burdens for years, whether emotional, spiritual, or mental, nothing you do seems to lighten the load. Even your best efforts leave you feeling drained. But I declare that God is lifting that weight now, in the name of Jesus.

Just as steam rising from an engine reveals that it's working properly, consistent gratitude shows that the soul is alive and functioning well. If you find yourself constantly struggling to be thankful, always reaching for joy or peace but rarely finding it, there may be unresolved trauma beneath the surface.

This is not something to overlook. It's important to recognize the signs of emotional trauma and to seek help when necessary. Sometimes, the healing begins by simply opening up, whether that's to a trusted person or to the Holy Spirit Himself. He is the ultimate Comforter and Counsellor. He will walk with you through the pain and lead you into truth.

IRRATIONAL RESPONSE TO LOVE

One of the clearest signs of unresolved trauma is how we respond to love.

"Love has been perfected among us in this: that we may have boldness in the day of judgment; because as He is, so are we in this world. There is no fear in love; but perfect love casts out fear, because fear involves torment. But he who fears has not been made perfect in love." (1 John 4:17–18)

When love is presented to you, does fear rise within you instead of peace? Do you find yourself second-guessing every act of kindness, every affectionate word? If someone buys you a cup of coffee, is your immediate thought, *"What do they want from me?"* When trauma is unresolved, suspicion becomes second nature. Your default setting shifts to defence mode even when no offence has occurred. It becomes hard to receive love for what it is because pain has trained you to prepare for betrayal.

Some even reject love altogether unless it is proven repeatedly, almost to the point of absurdity. Others go to the opposite extreme, clinging to every show of love, even when the Holy Spirit is nudging them with caution. Both reactions stem from the same root: fear. Fear of rejection, fear of abandonment, or fear of being deceived again.

If you constantly need to hear *"I love you,"* even after it's been spoken time and time again, it may not just be a desire for affection. It could be an indicator of emotional trauma. When love doesn't remain in your heart, when you forget it as quickly as it's given, something in the soul still needs healing.

And what about the fear of losing love? **Do you often find yourself imagining the death or departure of people who are still with you?** Does your mind race with thoughts of tragedy and separation, to the point where you feel the ache of loss long before it ever happens? That, too, is a symptom. You may be avoiding deep connection because you're afraid of how much it would hurt if it ever ended. But beloved, even a brief moment of true love is more valuable than a lifetime spent guarding yourself from it.

Love should not torment you neither should not scare you. If fear still lingers where love is present, then love has not yet been perfected in that area of your life. But healing is possible. God's desire is to make you whole so that you can receive love freely, give it generously, and walk in it boldly.

May you be healed of every wound that distorts your perception of love. May fear lose its grip on your heart. And may the perfect love of God cast out every remnant of torment, in the name of Jesus.

IRRATIONAL RESPONSE TO TRUTH

One of the clearest signs of unresolved trauma is how we respond when confronted with truth, especially when it comes through someone walking in the light.

"For you were once darkness, but now you are light in the Lord. Walk as children of light (for the fruit of the Spirit is in all goodness, righteousness, and truth), finding out what is acceptable to the Lord... But all things that are exposed are made manifest by the light, for whatever makes manifest is light." (Ephesians 5:8–13)

Light exposes. It doesn't just illuminate the path ahead, it reveals what's been hiding in our hearts. When you encounter someone who walks in purity and truth, it may feel inspiring, but it can also feel uncomfortable, especially if your soul has grown used to hiding in the shadows.

How do you respond when you witness healthy dynamics? Something genuinely godly? A faithful spouse; a loving, godly parent; a loyal friend who shows up no matter what.

If trauma still lingers, your first response may be skepticism. You might find yourself thinking, *"They must be faking it,"* or *"Nobody can be that pure."* Their smallest flaws become confirmation that they're not real, rather than reminders that they're human.

We see this in 2 Samuel 6:20, when David returned home after dancing before the Lord: *"Michal, the daughter of Saul, came out to meet him and said in disgust, 'How distinguished the king of Israel looked today, shamelessly exposing himself to the servant girls like any vulgar person might do!'"*

David's act was pure worship. But Michal, wounded by her own pain and insecurity, couldn't see it for what it was. His joy confronted her trauma and her reaction exposed her own broken lens.

This is why you must be careful who you allow to speak into your life. Not everyone's words are clean. Some are laced with unhealed pain, bitterness, or fear. When someone mocks your diligence in faith, your commitment to purity, or your honourable pursuit of God's design for relationships, understand that the issue is not your light, it's their wound.

Don't take advice from broken people. Take counsel from the Word of God.

Ask yourself: *"Is this wisdom drawn from Scripture, or from someone's disappointment?"* Not everyone conforms to the toxic patterns you've seen. God still has remnants who walk in truth, love well, and remain faithful.

When you see the light in someone else, don't let trauma make you suspicious, let it inspire you. Let it awaken the desire in you to be made whole. Truth is not your enemy. As a child of God, you are light in the Lord. Let truth of God's word challenge and refine you. And as you continue to heal, you'll find that the same light you once resisted now becomes the light you reflect.

IRRATIONAL RESPONSE TO SUFFERING, PAIN, AND CHALLENGES

Pain has a way of revealing whether you've been healed or simply functioning. When someone has been deeply wounded, even the slightest challenge can trigger a desire to retreat, escape or go back to what's familiar, even if it's dysfunctional.

This is exactly what we see in the children of Israel. Though God had delivered them from Egypt, Egypt had not yet been delivered from them. The trauma of slavery was still embedded in their hearts. So every time they faced discomfort, they cried out to return. *"It was better in Egypt,"* they said, forgetting the torment and the prayers they once prayed for freedom.

Trauma convinces you that past bondage is safer than present uncertainty. That's how you know healing hasn't taken root, when pain or the pursuit of pleasure drives your decisions instead of purpose.

"For it was fitting for Him, for whom are all things and by whom are all things, in bringing many sons to glory, to make the captain of their salvation perfect through sufferings." (Hebrews 2:10)

If Jesus, our perfect Saviour, was made perfect through suffering, why would we expect our journey to be any different? His suffering perfected Him. If yours is only breaking you, rather than building you, it may be because there's still a wound left unhealed.

Think of it like going to the gym. The pain of lifting weights is controlled and purposeful. But if something is already torn or injured, that same pressure causes damage instead of strength. When your pain always feels destructive rather than refining, it's time to ask, *"What in me still needs healing?"*

Ask yourself:

- Do you compromise your character when you feel attacked?

- Do you justify sin when you feel unappreciated, like Moses did in frustration?

- Are you quick to abandon your standards when lack sets in?

When suffering pushes you into behaviours that don't reflect who you are in Christ, it's not just weakness, it's often unresolved pain. Trauma makes you think, *"If I'm hurting, I'm allowed to sin."* But pain does not excuse disobedience. Instead, it should lead you back to the arms of the Father.

May God perfect you through your pain. And may every challenge become an opportunity for transformation, not regression.

Irrational Response to Being Ignored or Unappreciated

How do you respond when you feel ignored?

A healthy soul can remain steady even when attention is lacking. But when trauma is still present, being ignored whether its intentional or not can feel destabilizing. You might find yourself spiralling emotionally over something small, like someone not replying to your message or not greeting you in a hallway.

Some adults, though grown in age, still carry wounds that make them crave constant affirmation. If they're not being pampered, entertained, or acknowledged, they feel threatened. That's not immaturity, it's often unhealed trauma.

Someone once told me about an individual who couldn't handle being ignored. If she sent you a message and didn't get a reply quickly, she would start scrolling through your social media, trying to figure out if you were deliberately avoiding her. And if she saw that you posted something without replying to her first, she would get angry and accuse you of being intentionally dismissive. That's trauma talking. Because in truth, no one owes you a reply on your timeline.

Have you ever gone from a emotional high to a sudden crash, just because someone didn't respond to your *"hello?"* You walked into Church full of joy, but one ignored greeting shifted your entire mood. That's a sign something deeper is going on. Some people can brush it off— *"Oh, they probably didn't hear me."* But for others, it stings like rejection, and it sits. The next time that person greets them, they respond with coldness, trying to return the perceived offence.

Why is that? Because rejection trains us to interpret silence as abandonment. And if that wound has not been addressed, every present silence sounds like past rejection.

The Danger of Wrong Interpretations and Assumptions

Look at the Israelites in Exodus 32:1. Moses hadn't come down from the mountain yet, and they grew impatient. They said, *"As for this Moses, the man who brought us up out of Egypt, we do not know what has become of him."* So they turned to Aaron and said, *"Come, make us gods that shall go before us."* Did Moses tell them how long he would be gone? No. But their trauma couldn't handle the delay. They interpreted silence as abandonment and chose to fill the perceived gap with something else.

Sometimes, the problem isn't what happened, it's how we interpret what happened. Would you rather live in assumption, or seek out the truth? Some people assume the worst and call it discernment. But discernment doesn't default to suspicion, it searches for truth.

Many live by assumption. They assume people don't like them. They assume they're being avoided. They assume they're unwanted. And often, they never stop to ask if it's even true. Because trauma convinces them that asking might hurt more than assuming.

Even with God, some people are convinced He's angry with them. But they've never stopped to ask, *"Lord, are You pleased with me?"* That's how trauma works: it builds a wall between you and the truth and convinces you that it's safer not to know.

Some people can't imagine God correcting them. But He does. He's a loving Father, and love includes correction. Sometimes He'll say, *"Stop,"* not to reject you but to protect you. Just like you'd shout at someone about to walk into traffic.

Let's be honest, not everyone will love you, and that's okay. It's unrealistic to expect universal approval. But not everyone who doesn't speak to you is against you. Some are simply just quiet.

But if their hatred ever crosses into your domain, then they are playing with fire.

Additional Signs of Trauma

Emotional Instability

Frequent mood swings, intense emotional responses, and difficulty handling everyday stress can be signs that your soul is still wounded. If small issues trigger disproportionate reactions, something deeper may be calling for your attention. Trauma often leaves the nervous system in a heightened state, so what should be a bump in the road feels like a mountain crashing down.

Hyper-vigilance

Always being on edge, suspicious, or anxious, especially when there's no real threat, is another sign of trauma. Your mind and body are constantly in "survival mode," because your past pain has taught you that safety is never guaranteed. Even when things are peaceful, you can't relax. You're always bracing for the next blow.

Avoidant Behaviour

You might find yourself avoiding certain places, people, or conversations that remind you of painful experiences. While boundaries are wise, avoidance is rooted in fear. Trauma tries to shrink your world so that you never have to feel that pain again. But healing expands your capacity to live freely and fully.

Withdrawal

Some people isolate themselves, not because they're introverts, but because they're afraid. Afraid of being seen, known, or hurt again. You stop showing up in community. You avoid connection. But isolation is not safety, it's slow erosion. God created us for relationship. Healing requires re-engagement.

Intrusive Thoughts and Flashbacks

These are distressing and involuntary thoughts. You may be fully present in a moment, but suddenly, a memory barges in. You feel like you're right back in the trauma again. These flashbacks and thoughts often come without warning, and they can disrupt your day, your peace, and your faith.

We see this in the life of the prophet Jeremiah. After witnessing the destruction of Jerusalem, he cried out in Lamentations 3:19–20: *"Remember my affliction and roaming, the wormwood and the gall. My soul still remembers and sinks within me."*

Physical Symptoms

Sometimes your body says what your mouth won't. Headaches, muscle tension, stomach problems, can all be physical manifestations of internal conflict. King David described this after his sin and the weight of unconfessed guilt. In Psalms 38:6–8, he wrote: *"I am troubled, I am bowed down greatly; I go mourning all the day long. For my loins are full of inflammation, and there is no soundness in my flesh. I am feeble and severely broken; I groan because of the turmoil of my heart."*

Defensive Behaviour

If you have been hurt deeply, you may build emotional defences, sarcasm, withdrawal, hostility, not just to protect yourself, but to keep others out. You assume people are out to get you. You prepare for betrayal before it happens.

King Saul demonstrated this when he grew jealous of David. Even though David was loyal, Saul's insecurity turned to suspicion: *"Then Saul was very angry... 'What more can he have but the kingdom?' So Saul eyed David from that day forward."* (1 Samuel 18:8–9)

Unhealthy Coping Mechanisms

Trauma often drives people to medicate their pain through substances, distractions, overeating, or other patterns of escape. What starts as relief becomes bondage. King Solomon poured himself into pleasure and achievement, hoping to fill the void. But in Ecclesiastes 2:10–11, he confessed: *"Whatever my eyes desired I did not keep from them... Yet when*

I surveyed all that my hands had done... everything was meaningless, a chasing after the wind."

Relational Difficulties

When someone who is broken enters a relationship or marriage, their partner isn't just meeting a person, they're meeting every unhealed wound that still lives within them. It's not just love they'll be navigating, but layers of pain, triggers, and trauma. But I declare that you are being perfected and delivered, in the name of Jesus.

Trauma complicates connection. You may push people away because you don't trust them. Or you may cling too tightly, afraid of abandonment. Either way, relationships become fragile and strained.

We see this in David's relationship with Absalom. After deep family wounds, the Bible says: *"And the king said, 'Let him return to his own house, but do not let him see my face.' So Absalom returned to his own house, but did not see the king's face."* (2 Samuel 14:24)

Low Self-Esteem and Identity Issues

When trauma lingers, so does shame. You feel unworthy, dirty, inadequate. Even your victories can't silence the internal narrative that you're not enough.

Jeremiah, overwhelmed by the burden of his calling, cried out in Jeremiah 20:14, *"Cursed be the day in which I was born! Let the day not be blessed in which my mother bore me!"* This was identity trauma. The weight of pain distorted how he saw himself and his purpose.

Difficulty Experiencing Joy

When you've carried sorrow too long, joy can feel foreign. You may find yourself numb in moments that should feel sweet. Even laughter feels out of place.

Job, who endured unimaginable grief, said: *"For my sighing comes before I eat, and my groanings pour out like water... I am not at ease, nor am I quiet; I have no rest, for trouble comes."* (Job 3:24–26)

3

Traumatized by Your Cross

There are two kinds of trauma we experience in life. One is the result of human wickedness. The other is divinely permitted, woven into God's plan for our formation. If we fail to discern the difference, we risk rejecting our cross and forfeiting our destiny.

Some trauma is not caused by failure, sin, or even demonic attack, it's the weight of the assignment God placed on you. Obedience comes with a cost, and when the cross you're called to carry begins to wound you, it's not always a sign to retreat. Sometimes, it's confirmation that you're exactly where God wants you to be.

"Now there stood by the cross of Jesus His mother, and His mother's sister, Mary the wife of Clopas, and Mary Magdalene. When Jesus therefore saw His mother, and the disciple whom He loved standing by, He said to His mother, 'Woman, behold your son!'" (John 19:25-27)

Picture Mary at the foot of the cross, watching her Son—the One the angel said would save the world—bleeding and gasping for air. Imagine her waking up at night, heart racing, haunted by the memory: the blood, the agony, the helplessness, and the crushing reality that she could do nothing to stop it.

Have You Been Betrayed?

There are moments when trauma is not rooted in evil but birthed through purpose. If you can't put down the cross, you can't avoid the pain. And if you mislabel divine pain as a demonic attack, you may end up rejecting what God intended to use for His glory.

Jesus Himself wasn't spared. He lived under the shadow of a scandal no one would ever understand. People in His hometown likely mocked Him, saying, *"That's the boy whose mother said she was overshadowed by the Holy Spirit."*

Scripture shows us that betrayal was built into His journey: *"He who dipped his hand with Me in the dish will betray Me. The Son of Man indeed goes just as it is written of Him, but woe to that man by whom the Son of Man is betrayed! It would have been good for that man if he had not been born."* (Matthew 26:23–24)

This wasn't betrayal by a stranger. Judas had walked with Him, witnessed miracles, heard His teaching, and shared His meals, but still sold Him out for thirty pieces of silver. That's trauma. And yet, it was part of the plan.

The Test of Being Overlooked

Many have called me, saying, *"Apostle, I know I'm called. The calling of God is on me."* And I believe them—many are genuinely called. But calling alone is not enough. There is a process that cannot be skipped: **you must be ignored first**. That's death. If you can't be overlooked and still remain joyful, faithful, and submitted, then you're not ready. You may have the gift to preach, but you won't survive what comes after the preaching.

Sometimes, the most spiritual thing I can do is say nothing. Just watch to see if they will keep doing what God told them when there's no mic, no stage, no audience. That's where the making happens. It's not just about what you do in the light, it's about your posture while you are in the shadows.

WHEN PAIN ACCOMPANIES PURPOSE

I've had my share of difficult seasons, studying in Poland, working in Denmark, and adjusting to life in Toronto. None of it was easy. But looking back, I see the design. God had plans for me to be the prophet over Canada, and He was leading me here. Even the bullying I endured in boarding school became a gateway to reach those who've been wounded in ways words can't describe.

Still, I want to make it clear that not all pain is divine. A child being sexually abused is not the will of God. That is evil and demonic. And anyone who teaches otherwise is not speaking the heart of God. Yet even in the darkest of places, redemption is possible.

"All things work together for good to those who love God, to those who are the called according to His purpose." (Romans 8:28)

There are some crosses God Himself assigns. And when the trauma you're facing is part of that calling, He will give you the grace to endure. He won't let it crush you. He always provides a way forward, if your eyes are open to see it.

So if your pain feels connected to your purpose, don't rush to escape it. Ask God for discernment and let the Holy Spirit open your understanding. In business and systems analysis, we use "use cases" to examine scenarios from different lenses— for example, through the eyes of a user, a stakeholder, or a developer. In the same way, Scripture reveals deeper meaning when examined from different perspectives. A single verse can hold multiple layers of truth.

Take Joseph the carpenter. Even after Jesus' death, Roman crucifixions continued. Joseph likely kept building crosses—the very tool used to execute his Son. Imagine him coming home, and Mary asking, *"How was your day?"* To which he might reply, *"I built another cross."* What kind of pain would that stir in her heart? And yet, maybe Joseph gently reminded her: *"He's not just your Son anymore. He's our Saviour. And He's alive."*

The very cross that traumatized them became the tool that saved us. As Jesus said,*"He who lives by the sword shall die by the sword."* (Matthew 26:52) If you were raised to handle snakes, expect to be bitten. If you're called to carry a cross, don't be surprised when it draws blood.

Trauma by Design

We've delved into the idea that trauma can accompany the pursuit of purpose, but it can be deeper than that. Some traumas are woven into your nature even before you started pursuing your assignment. Some traumas are not the result of obedience or action. They are part of your construction. The way you process emotion, the things you're sensitive to, the rejection you've always felt but couldn't explain—these are evidence of the particular kind of grace you carry.

For some, the trauma is rooted in temperament: deep empathy, unusual sensitivity, or a constant sense of being misunderstood. For others, it's familial—generational patterns, childhood instability, or a tendency to carry burdens that aren't theirs. But in every case, the trauma is not incidental. It is embedded.

God does not just prepare people for ministry; He builds ministers for a specific kind of pain. The trauma, in this case, is not just shaping your purpose, it is part of your design.

Jesus once said to the crowd, *"Have you come out as against a robber with swords and clubs to take Me? I sat daily with you, teaching in the temple, and you did not seize Me. But all this was done that the Scriptures of the prophets might be fulfilled."* (Matthew 26:55-56) Then, all His disciples forsook Him and fled. It was not chaos, it was design.

If you've ever felt completely rejected, perhaps that's a mark of your prophetic calling. I've never encountered a true prophet who didn't endure seasons of abandonment and isolation. A wilderness season is not optional, it's essential. You can't skip it. When you understand that, you stop praying it away and start asking God for grace—not grace to resist it, but grace to endure and steward it well.

Demons don't communicate, yet the rejection pattern follows you. Parents whisper warnings about you to other parents, based on nothing but a feeling. And you are left wondering, *"What do they see in me?"* Yet, you might have the most tender, genuine heart. But it's by design.

Have you ever found yourself confessing just to keep the peace, even when you knew you were innocent? Do you move cities, countries, relationships, and still encounter the same rejection? That's not coincidence. It's design.

Jesus carried the sin of the world to become our righteousness. That meant He was blamed for things He didn't do. Likewise, some of us have spent our lives being misunderstood, falsely accused, and blamed for things we never did. But that, too, may be part of God's plan. To become a true advocate, you need to know the pain of injustice firsthand. It gives you eyes to see beyond appearances and into the truth. Today, one accusation is often enough to destroy a person. The world doesn't pause to ask questions. But when you've been falsely accused yourself, you start to respond differently. You start to say, *"Hold on, what if they're not guilty?"*

"He made Him who knew no sin to be sin for us." (2 Corinthians 5:21)

On the cross, Jesus didn't look holy. He looked like the worst of humanity—a liar, a thief, a predator—because He carried the weight of our sin. Some people, through no fault of their own, carry the same burden. They're seen as the problem wherever they go.

The Principle of Polarity

In the Kingdom of God, the way up is always down.

People admire the anointing on Benny Hinn's life, but few know the hardship he endured. Rejected, beaten, misunderstood, yet is now celebrated and honoured globally. His testimony, like many others, proves that the oil only flows where there has been crushing.

A healing evangelist may face relentless health challenges. A prophet may be buried in seasons of isolation. A kingdom financier may first know poverty. Each calling comes with a cross.

I remember the Lord telling me, *"Let this be the last time you ask for anything when people come to Church or a conference. You are a servant. Your job is to make sure they receive everything I've prepared for them."* That changed my posture. So when people disrespect me, I understand. I'm not here for me. As a pastor, I don't come with my own agenda, I carry yours. You still want to be a pastor? Then welcome the design.

"When He ascended on high, He led captivity captive, and gave gifts to men. (Now this, 'He ascended'—what does it mean but that He also first descended into the lower parts of the earth?)" (Ephesians 4:8-10)

Jesus

Jesus had to descend before He could ascend. The glory we now celebrate came through the path of suffering and surrender. He had to go low to be lifted high. And some of us must be taken down—stripped of visibility, comfort, and affirmation—because that's the only road to glory.

And when God allows you to descend first, it doesn't only affect you. Your loved ones feel it too.

John

Picture John the Baptist's parents being asked, *"Where's your son?"*

"He's in the wilderness."

"What wilderness?"

"We don't really know. He checks in when he's ready."

Then they see him—gaunt, wild-eyed, eating locusts and honey. Would you introduce someone like that to your guests? Probably not. But when John stepped out and began baptizing multitudes, calling people to repentance, everything changed. The shame turned to honour. The silence turned to recognition. But before the fruit, there was misunderstanding, pain, and isolation.

Sometimes even well-meaning parents try to rescue us from the wilderness God led us into. They say, *"Just get your degree so we can introduce you properly."* But when the evidence of your calling shows, they'll say, *"That's my child. I always knew they'd make it."*

Light Hidden In Darkness

Some revelation is hidden in pain, some buried in sickness and others lie behind dark doors. If you want the honey, you'll need to brave the beehive.

Paul understood this tension well. *"Lest I should be exalted above measure by the abundance of revelations, a thorn in the flesh was given to me—a messenger of Satan to buffet me."* (2 Corinthians 12:7) The thorn was by design. It came packaged with the revelation. Many want the glory, but not the groaning. But you cannot have the crown without the cross. Some insights live in demonic territory. You must go in, retrieve them, and bring them out. But it costs you.

There was a time you couldn't even say *"meditation"* in Church. Some of us had to go into dark places and bring that word back. We were called heretics and devil worshippers. But we kept preaching, quoting Scripture, and standing our ground. And slowly, the light came back.

The same will happen with other truths. But hear this: **every revelation you carry comes with a fight**. If you're called to bring light, expect to battle darkness. But once the darkness fades, they'll see the light you were carrying all along.

I remember a man of God in Africa who received deep insight about the anointing oil. He wrote a book. Another respected leader tore it up on national TV and called it heresy. Years later, that same critic began preaching the same revelation, and thanked the man he once attacked.

If you want to be great, don't expect everyone to love you. *"Woe to you when all men speak well of you."* (Luke 6:26) Sometimes, to stay blessed, you might need to pay people to hate you.

Do You Want to Be Great?

Joseph was thrown into prison for something he didn't do, by design. What was he doing in prison when he did nothing to deserve it? He may not have deserved it his destiny required it.

The desire for greatness often comes with a price—significant challenges and prolonged suffering. Throughout Scripture, every person who achieved greatness did so through perseverance and unwavering faith in the midst of adversity.

Consider Moses. Born into a time of oppression, he faced rejection, exile, and hardship. He led a stubborn people through the wilderness for forty years. His journey was not glamorous, but it was necessary. And through that process, God raised him as a prophet and a deliverer.

"By faith Moses, when he became of age, refused to be called the son of Pharaoh's daughter, choosing rather to suffer affliction with the people of God than to enjoy the passing pleasures of sin." (Hebrews 11:24–25)

If you truly want to be great, you must be ready to endure trials that do not make sense at first. Greatness requires the ability to keep going when nothing around you affirms your calling. It requires trust in God's plan, even when the process feels like punishment.

Nothing great comes without pressure. Think of the process behind premium Japanese knives—heat, pressure, folding, refining. That's what makes them valuable. God desires uniqueness in His people, but many opt for mediocrity because it's easier. Becoming one-of-a-kind is costly. And some only realize it when they see the price wasn't for quality alone, but for rarity.

Paying the Price of Greatness

The process of building a purpose-driven life is costly. Trauma is part of it.

In the days of Esther, the young women were placed under the care of eunuchs—men who could be trusted not to defile what they were assigned to prepare. That's a picture of what God does in us. He allows us to die to the things we want to have dominion over. The process isn not to harm you—it's to protect what you're being called to carry. Before God gives you influence, He'll test your restraint.

You want to lead crowds? First, you must learn to walk alone. You want your name known? Then you must master how to serve without a name.

During years of loneliness, I read books on psychology without knowing why. I was just reading, gathering insight and growing spiritually. But God already knew part of the ministry would be raising emotionally healthy people. I did not understand it then, but now I see that season for what it was: divine investment. The Lord told me, *"It is more powerful to heal a person's emotions than to heal their body."*

Try finding someone who can heal schizophrenia or trauma with medication. It doesn't exist. But God said, *"I've made you for a time such as this."* Many people came to the Church broken, but the Lord used me as a vessel to piece them back together. Now they can minister with strength and deliver the Word with clarity—all because my emotional healing power came by design.

So when the enemy tries to remind you of what you went through, laugh. Speak back and say, *"This pain was not wasted. It's working for my good."* No pain, no gain. The highest life only comes from the deepest death.

Some of us have died many times. And you don't even know it's death until you're in a situation where you can't pull yourself out. That's when the power of God lifts you. That's how you know it was by design.

I remember a woman who now makes cakes that bless the world. When we first met, I saw her at Starbucks—carrying heaviness, practically dead on the inside. But God revived her. And now anyone who eats her cake will tell you: it carries life. The same woman the enemy tried to bury is now feeding others with what was birthed through pain.

Let me be clear: I am not referring to suicide. If you take your own life, that's destruction. There's no blessing in that. But when God Himself takes you through death—death to pride, to ambition, to self—and you trust Him in the process, He will raise you up. You'll walk through the valley of the shadow of death, but you won't fear. Why? Because *He* is with you.

"Though I walk through the valley of the shadow of death, I will fear no evil; for You are with me." (Psalms 23:4)

Discernment: Which Pain is Part of Your Purpose?

Discernment in the kingdom is not just about identifying good versus evil—it's about recognizing whether your pain is an attack from the enemy or a necessary component of your calling. One pain requires resistance while the other requires surrender. Wisdom is knowing the difference.

When Jesus told His disciples that He would be betrayed and crucified, Peter immediately pushed back: *"Don't say that!"* he insisted. But Jesus rebuked him sharply: *"Get behind Me, Satan! You do not have in mind the concerns of God, but merely human concerns."* (Matthew 16:23)

Peter was not trying to sabotage Jesus, he simply lacked discernment. He didn't understand that the pain Jesus was about to endure was not a tragedy but a divine necessity. Even Jesus, in Gethsemane, felt the weight of this design. *"My soul is exceedingly sorrowful, even to death. Stay here and watch with Me... O My Father, if it is possible, let this cup pass from Me; nevertheless, not as I will, but as You will."* (Matthew 26:38–39)

There are people who have to be fired seven times before the door to destiny opens. Some of the most impactful voices today were forged in fire. Malala Yousafzai was shot in the face simply because she was advocating for girls in Pakistan to go to school. That kind of trauma doesn't look like favour at first glance. But today, presidents and prime ministers line up to shake her hand. That bullet didn't break her, it revealed the weight of her assignment.

The devil is often part of the package, but not always in the way we think. Discernment means knowing which challenge is an attack to resist and which one is a fire to submit to. You may be praying for deliverance when God is preparing your platform through endurance. Knowing the difference is everything.

Being married is not always a sign that God is pleased with someone. I've had conversations with people who assumed marriage was automatically God's reward. I've asked some directly, *"Are you convinced the Lord wants you to be married?"* And after a moment of honest reflection, they've said, *"Maybe not."* And I tell them plainly, *"Let me confirm it for you. It's not in your destiny to be married."*

You see, for some people, being unmarried is not a limitation. God knows the assignment He's given you, and for some, that assignment requires a level of focus and freedom that marriage would disrupt. It doesn't make you less blessed. It means your blessing looks different. And when they accept it, not begrudgingly, but joyfully, they find a grace to run in their lane with power. That's what discernment produces: peace in the midst of divine difference.

I once had ambitions of becoming president of the World Bank. That was my plan. But God had another. He redirected me into ministry, and it came with its own pain. The kind that's misunderstood and invites criticism. I've learned to ask, *"Lord, is this pain from You? If it is, I'll settle in."*

You may pray for others and see instant results. But when you pray for yourself, nothing happens. Don't be discouraged. It could be that the anointing on your life comes with restraints to keep you yielded. It's not punishment—it's preservation.

Recognizing Trauma You Should Allow

This is how you know trauma is by design: God is still with you in it. His presence doesn't always remove the pain, but it transforms how you walk through it. Even in the darkest valleys, the fruit of the Spirit continues to flow— *"love, joy, peace, patience, kindness, goodness, faithfulness, gentleness, and self-control."* (Galatians 5:22)

These qualities are evidence that God is present with you and that you are still aligned with His will, even when your life doesn't yet look like a testimony. Yes, you may need to stay connected to the channels of grace more than you usually would to remain strengthened. But the very fact that you can endure with peace, remain kind, or still love others is proof that grace is holding you up until glory breaks through.

In the kingdom, the way up is always down. And what looks like a setback might be the starting point of your greatest elevation. What appears to be a major loss could be the seed of a generational breakthrough. That's why you must be careful—because the thing you're tempted to despise may be the very thing God is using to lift you. It takes discernment to say, *"Lord, I don't like this, but if it's You, I'll stay under it until the glory shows."*

Don't curse what God is using to crown you. The wrapping may look ugly, but the gift inside is divine. Discernment will help you maintain the right heart posture when the process is hard.

Prayer

"Lord, I need discernment. Help me separate the pain that is by Your design from the pain that comes from the enemy. Open my understanding. Show me which challenges I need to resist, and which ones I need to endure with grace. Let me not mislabel divine process as satanic attack. Keep my heart soft. Keep my posture right. Let me not complain my way out of a cross You assigned to crown me. In Jesus' mighty name, I pray. Amen."

EMBRACE THE DESIGN WITH JOY

With accurate discernment and proper perspective, joy becomes the response to trials.

"Father, I thank You, because now I understand that being called as a prophet comes with the pain of abandonment. I give You praise, because what once felt like rejection—being abandoned by family, forsaken by close friends, and falsely accused—was all part of Your divine design. And for that, I give You thanks."

This understanding allows you to carry your cross with confidence, boldness, and a smile, knowing that your journey is divinely orchestrated. Embrace the trials as part of God's plan, and you'll find joy, strength, and purpose in every step.

4

Trauma From Within the Church

The Church was designed to be a safe haven, a place where the wounded could come and find healing. A place where the broken are restored. But sadly, that's not always the case. In fact, for many, it has been far from that. Lord, help us.

The Bible says judgment will begin in the house of God and there's good reason for that. The house of God should be the first place where love, justice, and mercy flow. It's meant to be a sanctuary for the hurting, a refuge for the weary.

But imagine someone running from danger, an attacker or abuser, and finding a city of refuge, only to be violated again within its gates. Where is the hope in that? I read about someone who fled the war in Ukraine only to be stabbed in Ontario, Canada. That's what it feels like when someone escapes pain out in the world, only to find more pain within the Church. And many begin to wonder, *"Is it me? Am I the one with the problem?"*

There are many reasons people have experienced trauma within the Church—and we will walk through them in this chapter. As we touch on these painful experiences, I encourage you to let your memories rise to the surface. Don't suppress them again. Let them come up so they can be permanently dealt with.

As I preached a message on trauma, many people began to cry as old wounds were exposed. It was the Spirit of God bringing healing. If that happens as you read, let the tears flow. And most importantly, choose to forgive. Say it out loud: *"Lord, I forgive them."*

Forgiveness is a deliberate act. It is not passive. You say it, you decide it: *"I forgive this person. I forgive that person."* As Colossians 3:13 says, *"Bear with each other and forgive one another if any of you has a grievance against someone. Forgive as the Lord forgave you."*

WOLVES IN SHEEP'S CLOTHING

Some of the deepest wounds come from those we least expect, from within the Church. From people meant to guide and shepherd us, but who instead exploit, deceive, and harm. The Bible calls them wolves in sheep's clothing. Outwardly, they appear righteous. But inside, they are dangerous.

Jesus warned us in Matthew 7:15: *"Beware of false prophets, who come to you in sheep's clothing, but inwardly they are ravening wolves."* These individuals can leave behind deep emotional and spiritual trauma, causing confusion, disillusionment, and even a crisis of faith.

Identifying these wolves takes discernment, wisdom, and a strong relationship with God. We must judge them by their fruit, not just their words. If someone charges for prophecy, if they demand money before ministering to you, run. That is not of God. You can sow seeds and give offerings as an act of worship. But when it's coerced, when they say, *"You must bring a prophet's offering,*" it is false. Elijah didn't require a fee. Neither did Samuel. Saul sought guidance from Samuel, and no money was involved.

"By their fruits you shall know them. Do men gather grapes of thorns, or figs of thistles? Even so, every good tree brings forth good fruit; but a corrupt tree brings forth evil fruit... Therefore, by their fruits you shall know them." (Matthew 7:16–20)

It's not about being perfect. But an orange tree cannot produce poison. If you've been exposed to that kind of manipulation and control, may the Lord deliver you now.

THE CHURCH IS NOT A CULT

The Church was never meant to be a place of abuse. We don't even need to revisit the horrific accounts of clergy misconduct or manipulative online prophets—tragically, those stories have become all too common.

One woman reached out to a "prophet" desperate for deliverance. He told her that her freedom required sexual intercourse with him. Thank God she spoke up and someone intervened. When people are desperate, they can be easily deceived. Some are told that praying in the name of Jesus isn't enough, and are made to do absurd things, jump like a frog fifteen times, crawl, or act out rituals. It is clearly manipulation.

In some Churches, giving has been weaponized. An offering bowl is placed at the centre during a dance, made of metal so the sound of coins draws attention. It pressures people to give, not out of love, but out of shame. This too, creates trauma.

There are also leaders who twist the message of authority and use it to control lives. Let's be clear: spiritual authority is first the Word of God. Then the Holy Spirit within you. Then human authority.

No one has the right to speak abusively to you. You are Jesus' prized possession. If someone has spoken harsh words, they should be corrected. How much more serious is physical abuse? It must never happen.

Serving in the Church should be a joy, not a bondage. If someone decides not to serve, they should be free to follow through with that decision. The Church is not a cult. It is not here to control your money, your body, or your life.

Unintentional Wolves

Not everyone who causes harm in the Church is malicious. Some are what I would call "unintentional wolves." These are individuals who, though sincere, are sincerely wrong. Often driven by ignorance or misguided zeal, they can cause real damage without even realizing it. Their intentions may be good, but without maturity, knowledge, or fruit, their actions can wound just as deeply as those of someone acting with malice.

This happens when people are elevated into leadership based solely on their gifts. A talented preacher might deliver a moving message but there's no fruit. No character or depth. And when talent is exalted over spiritual maturity, trauma is often the outcome.

Preaching is only a small part of my calling as a pastor. It's not about stringing together impressive words or dazzling a crowd with speech. Ministry goes far beyond performance. When people are placed in positions of influence without spiritual fruit, the result can be devastating.

1 Timothy 3 outlines the qualifications for Church leadership and none of them have to do with talent. It's all about character. If you've been in a setting where leaders were chosen based on their money, their connections, or their charisma you were likely in a breeding ground for trauma.

In Acts 8:9–24, we read about Simon the sorcerer. He believed in Christ and was even baptized, yet he tried to buy spiritual power from the apostles. That's why it's so important to have clear criteria for serving in the house of God. Not to create barriers, but to ensure spiritual readiness. People like Simon may believe but they still need transformation. And until that happens, they shouldn't be placed in positions that can harm others.

Zealous People Without Knowledge

Another source of trauma in the Church comes from people who are full of zeal but empty of understanding. Their fire is real, but it is misdirected.

I've seen pastors hurt by their own members. But I have made up my mind that I will not be traumatized by anyone. However, if you're not grounded in your identity in Christ, it can shake you. People will try to make you feel guilty for being blessed.

Someone once told me that God was angry because my wife and I had different chairs from the rest of the congregation. Imagine that. They had no idea how those chairs came to be, how we were forced by God into that setup. They just showed up and judged. That's zeal without knowledge.

People see a carpet at the altar and say, *"See, this is unbiblical."* They don't know that we kneel down for hours, and the carpet is to ease the strain. They don't know we are in every service. They don't see the whole picture.

Romans 10:1–4 says, *"Brethren, my heart's desire and prayer to God for Israel is that they may be saved. For I bear them witness that they have a zeal for God, but not according to knowledge."* Zeal without knowledge becomes legalism. It becomes judgment. It becomes spiritual abuse.

People who don't understand the full story often make snap judgments. They see someone dressed a certain way on their first Sunday and assume the worst, never realizing it's their very first time stepping into a Church.

I remember someone accusing a woman of exploiting God's people because she launched a Christian program that wasn't free. They didn't consider the costs she was covering—Amazon Web Services, web hosting, logistics. They just assumed. People serve God with sincerity, and others tear them down from a distance.

Galatians 6:1 gives us the blueprint: *"Brethren, if a man is overtaken in any trespass, you who are spiritual restore such a one in a spirit of gentleness, considering yourself lest you also be tempted."*

Zeal without knowledge leads to hurt, judgment, and exclusion The goal should always be restoration, not humiliation. If you've been wounded by overzealous but under-taught people, may the Lord restore your heart. And may we all walk with both fire and wisdom, zeal and knowledge.

Wrong Responses to Sin and Error

Another source of trauma within the Church is how sin and mistakes are sometimes mishandled. When a member stumbles, the response should be marked by love, grace, and truth. But all too often, what people encounter is harshness, legalism, and condemnation, which only deepens their wounds.

Think of the woman caught in adultery. The religious leaders brought her to Jesus, ready to stone her. But Jesus' response was not harsh—it was holy. *"He who is without sin among you, let him throw a stone at her first."* (John 8:7) One by one, her accusers dropped their stones. Jesus then said, *"Neither do I condemn you; go and sin no more."* (John 8:11)

That is how we must respond, with both grace and truth.

But mishandling sin doesn't always mean harshness. Sometimes, the error is in covering things up or refusing to confront what's wrong. When serious wrongdoing, especially abuse, is ignored or excused, the trauma only grows deeper. Mercy for one person must never come at the cost of another's safety. As leaders, workers, and members of the body of Christ, we must discern when firm action is necessary, especially when minors or vulnerable individuals are involved.

OTHER EXAMPLES OF TRAUMA WITHIN THE CHURCH

Unnecessarily High Standards for Pastor's Kids

Growing up as a pastor's child, I saw it firsthand. Other children could make mistakes. But we were expected to be perfect. That pressure was suffocating. It forced us into pretence instead of allowing space to grow like normal kids. I had to confront this in myself and choose freedom or I would've stayed trapped in performance.

When People Leave a Church

Another trauma comes when someone leaves a Church and is treated as if they've abandoned Christ entirely. That assumption can lead to deep emotional pain. But the same God who led you to that Church can also lead you out. And when He does, and you move to a different Church, it's not rebellion against the Church or its leaders but it's obedience to God's instruction.

Borrowing Money Among Church Members

Let me be honest—there were times people borrowed money from me and never paid it back. Then, to make matters worse, they spread lies, questioned my beliefs, and tried to discredit the Church. That kind of betrayal runs deep.

One man took the money I knew I'd never see again, then turned around and argued that women shouldn't be on stage. I tried to explain, but he was too rooted in certain teachings. He left, kept the money, and spread lies that our Church didn't believe in the Bible.

You've probably seen this too. When people who receive help turn around slander the ones who helped them. Even if the pastor isn't directly involved, it still reflects on the Church, and you're left wondering, *"Why are Church people like this?"*

In another Church, a man gained sympathy through emotional stories, collected money, and vanished, only to repeat the same thing elsewhere. Situations like these make people hesitant to trust again. The Church, meant to be a place of love, becomes a place of betrayal.

That's why boundaries matter. Not from fear, but from wisdom. Even David knew the sting of betrayal and the importance of guarding his heart.

Release the Pain

Wherever you are right now, bow your head and speak to the Lord. It's okay to admit that some of your habits, routines, or even relationships have been shaped by past pain, especially from Church.

Let it go and forgive them.

When Jesus hung on the Cross, He said, *"Father, forgive them, for they know not what they do."* (Luke 23:34) We are called to follow His example. Forgive those who falsely accused you. Forgive those who mishandled your pain. Forgive those who assassinated your character or spread lies. And forgive yourself too. If you don't, guilt will weigh you down like a chain.

Our Heavenly Father has already forgiven you. So extend that same forgiveness for every rejection, every abandonment, every offence.

The Church belongs to Jesus. And even though human beings are flawed, don't let that stop you from loving Jesus or His Church. Forgive the one who shared what you told them in private and then used it in a sermon to target you. Forgive the leaders who showed favouritism, passing you over even though you were more qualified, simply because someone else gave more money.

"Bear with each other and forgive one another if any of you has a grievance against someone. Forgive as the Lord forgave you." (Colossians 3:13)

Despite its flaws, the Church is still the greatest institution on Earth. There is no other gathering like it. And if you cling to trauma, you might project that pain onto others and miss out on the love and community God has for you.

If you've genuinely been wounded by someone in the Church, please accept this heartfelt apology. Church leaders are doing their best to fulfill a holy assignment, but they are still human. They cannot see or know everything. But once an issue is brought to light, it must be handled with care and responsibility.

Forgiveness is the key. It unlocks your healing and allows you to walk in the fullness of God's love. Let Him mend your heart. Let Him restore your trust. And let Him lead you deeper into intimacy with Himself and fellowship with His Church.

5

The Journey of Deliverance

WHY IT IS IMPORTANT TO DEAL WITH TRAUMA

Ignoring trauma can have detrimental effects that ripple through various aspects of life. Understanding the importance of addressing trauma is essential for motivation and commitment to the healing process. Trauma can severely hamper personal development by instilling fears, self-doubt, and limiting beliefs. Imagine a tree planted in unsuitable soil. Its growth is stunted, and it can bear no fruit. Similarly, a traumatized individual might struggle to reach their full potential. By addressing trauma, one can nurture personal growth and achieve new heights.

Trauma often leads to strained relationships. Recognizing and dealing with trauma enhances your ability to form healthy, meaningful connections. The story of Joseph in the Bible highlights this importance. Betrayed by his brothers and sold into slavery, Joseph's journey of dealing with his trauma eventually led him to forgive his brothers and restore his familial relationships (Genesis 45:1-15).

Prolonged trauma can lead to chronic mental health issues like depression, anxiety, and PTSD, as well as physical symptoms such as headaches, fatigue, and chronic pain. Addressing trauma promotes overall well-being. Scripture reminds us, *"Beloved, I pray that you may prosper in all things and be in health, just as your soul prospers."* (3 John 1:2)

Trauma can shake one's faith and spiritual foundations. Healing from trauma enhances spiritual growth and helps you align more closely with your purpose and faith. Job, a man of great faith, experienced profound trauma. His journey of faith through suffering eventually led to a stronger relationship with God and restoration. (Job 42:1-6, 10-17) *"The Lord is near to those who have a broken heart, and saves such as have a contrite spirit."* (Psalms 34:18) May the Lord strengthen you and enable you to keep aiming for complete healing from every form of trauma.

DELIVERANCE STARTS WITH YOU

Deliverance from trauma begins with a crucial step: self-awareness. This involves recognizing the presence of trauma in your life, understanding its impact, and having the willingness to confront it head on. Acknowledging the reality that you need deliverance is the first step. Admit that it affected you, regardless of pride or cultural notions about keeping things inside. Dealing with trauma is not a sign of weakness but rather a step towards enjoy the best of God's design for your life.

A common barrier to this crucial step is denial which is the reluctance to admit that one has been impacted by trauma. Overcoming this denial requires bravery and honesty. Take time to reflect on past events and how they have affected your emotions, thoughts, and behaviours. Journaling about your feelings and experiences can clarify your thoughts and reveal patterns.

Additionally, seeking divine guidance through prayer and meditation can provide comfort and insight. Scripture encourages us to cast our anxieties on Him, *"casting all your care upon Him, for He cares for you."* (1 Peter 5:7) In 2 Corinthians 5:17, we are reminded, *"Therefore, if anyone is in Christ, he is a new creation; old things have passed away; behold, all things have become new."* This verse underscores the transformative power of becoming new in Christ, but it also highlights the need for ongoing renewal and healing. Spiritual rebirth does not automatically erase past traumas; intentional efforts must be made to address and heal from them.

Consider the biblical character, King David. Despite being anointed as the future king of Israel, he faced severe trials, including incessant persecution by King Saul. David's healing journey started with understanding that while he was supposed to have been joyful and excited for his upcoming coronation, he was sad and disquieted within himself. This self-awareness made him seek God's guidance, which eventually led to his deliverance. As Psalms 42:5 says, *"Why are you cast down, O my soul? And why are you disquieted within me? Hope in God; For I shall yet praise Him, the help of my countenance and my God."*

Deliverance vs. Freedom

While deliverance involves the initial act of being set free from trauma, freedom refers to the ongoing state of living without the constraints of past traumas. Deliverance is often a momentary or short-term event, whereas freedom involves staying permanently free. Understanding the difference between the two is crucial for setting realistic expectations. Deliverance focuses on removing immediate burdens, while freedom emphasizes the need continuous personal growth and the practice of disciplines that will keep you free. Why many experience frustration is that they were expecting to feel the way they felt when they were delivered every single day without putting in the work to stay free.

Sustaining freedom involves engaging in regular activities that promote mental, emotional, and spiritual health. Community support is essential; regular fellowship with supportive friends, family, or faith communities can provide encouragement. Developing new, healthy routines helps in reinforcing a life free from trauma's hold. Scripture's injunction is to *"stand fast therefore in the liberty by which Christ has made us free, and do not be entangled again with a yoke of bondage."* (Galatians 5:1) This Scripture underscores the importance of remaining steadfast in the freedom we have received.

6

Deliverance From Trauma

How Do We Get Restored?

The Bible makes it clear that it is our knowledge of the truth that makes us free (John 8:32). Restoration starts with truth that renews the mind and realigns the heart.

Think about when Jesus raised Lazarus from the dead. The moment Jesus called, *"Lazarus, come forth,"* was the quickest and simplest part of the whole process. But telling the people to roll away the stone, and later, *"Loose him, and let him go,"* were the difficult parts. The part Jesus had to play was the easiest. It was the people who struggled with the instructions.

That's often how restoration works. God is always ready to usher us into greater freedom but are we ready to obey? Will we let Him by submitting to His process?

One of the clearest examples of restoration from trauma in the Bible is found in John 8:1–11. It shows just how simple healing can be if we don't complicate it.

"But Jesus went to the Mount of Olives. Now early in the morning He came again into the temple, and all the people came to Him; and He sat down and taught them. Then the scribes and Pharisees brought to Him a woman caught in adultery. And when they had set her in the midst, they said to Him, 'Teacher, this woman was caught in adultery, in the very act. Now Moses, in the law, commanded us that such should be stoned. But what do You say?' This they said, testing Him, that they might have something of which to accuse Him. But Jesus stooped down and wrote on the ground with His finger, as though He did not hear. So when they continued asking Him, He raised Himself up and said to them, 'He who is without sin among you, let him throw a stone at her first.' And again He stooped down and wrote on the ground. Then those who heard it, being convicted by their conscience, went out one by one, beginning with the oldest even to the last. And Jesus was left alone, and the woman standing in the midst. When Jesus had raised Himself up and saw no one but the woman, He said to her, 'Woman, where are those accusers of yours? Has no one condemned you?' She said, 'No one, Lord.' And Jesus said to her, 'Neither do I condemn you; go and sin no more.'" (John 8:1–11)

In this story, it wasn't just Jesus there. The Bible says *all the people came to Him, and He sat down and taught them.* Imagine it like a Church service where Jesus was in the middle of teaching, and suddenly, the scribes and Pharisees barged in, dragging this woman into the crowd.

Imagine the level of shame she must have felt. It's one thing to be caught in sin, but it's another thing entirely to be dragged into public, into Church, and have your mistake exposed in front of everyone. There was no opportunity to defend herself and the law didn't give her a voice. On top of the trauma of the act itself, she was now facing the trauma of public humiliation and the threat of death. But look at how quick, how deep, and how complete her restoration was. Jesus confronted the accusers, and one by one, they dropped their stones and walked away, convicted by their own conscience. When everyone had left, He turned to her and said, *"Woman, where are those accusers of yours? Has no one condemned you?"*

And this was the first and only time she spoke in the whole process. She said, *"No one, Lord."*

Some people believe the process of restoration must be long and exhausting. But it doesn't always have to be. It can be this simple. Jesus replied, *"Neither do I condemn you. Go and sin no more."* And immediately, He said those words, the shame was gone, the risk of death was gone, and this woman was restored to the state she was in before the adultery.

From this story we can draw the steps to restoration.

Step 1: Admit That You Are Traumatized

In the story of the woman caught in adultery, she didn't argue or make excuses when Jesus asked her, *"Where are your accusers?"* She simply accepted the situation.

Admitting that you are traumatized doesn't mean you are throwing the person who caused it under the bus, especially when it is someone close to you, like a father, mother, or sibling. It's complex, because you love this person, yet they caused you pain. And for many, it feels disloyal to even acknowledge the trauma.

But healing starts with truth. When dealing with trauma:

- Acknowledge that the traumatic event happened, and that it affected you deeply.

- Understand that you cannot deal with everything all at once; healing is a process.

- Be prepared for different aspects of the trauma to surface over time.

Admitting that you are traumatized is simple, but it is not optional. It doesn't mean your world will collapse; in fact, it means your healing can finally begin. By acknowledging the pain, you open the door for God to bring healing and restoration.

"There is no fear in love. But perfect love drives out fear, because fear has to do with punishment. The one who fears is not made perfect in love." (1 John 4:18)

Admitting you are traumatized takes sincerity and humility. Saying something like, *"Yes, I was molested as a child,"* is a powerful act of admission. When Jesus said to the woman, *"Where are your accusers?"* that statement carried weight. And her response, *"No one, Lord"* was an admission. She didn't deny what happened. In essence, she was saying, "Yes, I was caught in the act. I have no defence. I admit it."

Step 2: Recount the Traumatic Incident

Recounting the traumatic incident is a key part of deliverance.

In the Old Testament, when the Israelites sinned in the wilderness, God allowed venomous snakes to afflict them. When they cried out for mercy, the Lord instructed Moses to create a bronze serpent and raise it on a pole. It was snake versus snake. And God said that whoever looked at it would live. That is a picture of healing, when you look at what hurt you.

To deal with trauma, you must revisit the place where the pain happened, not physically, but in conversation. You have to face the same snake that bit you, but this time, you are not alone.

Deciding who to open up to

When it comes to recounting trauma, choose your confidant wisely. Just because you feel emotionally connected to someone in the moment does not mean they are the right person to open up to. Do not confuse closeness for safety.

Dealing with trauma is spiritual surgery. And just like you would not allow just anyone to operate on your physical body, you should not entrust just anyone with your inner wounds. Sharing your trauma will place you in a vulnerable position. Make sure the person you speak to is spiritually mature, emotionally stable, and knows how to carry your story with grace and confidentiality.

Ideally, it should not be the same person who hurt you, unless they are now truly walking under the grace of God. Even then, discern the spirit they carry. If they come with defensiveness or a need to argue, what was meant to be a moment of healing can quickly become a battlefield.

You can also recount your experience with the Holy Spirit. In fact, some people prefer this route, especially when they are not ready to talk to anyone else. And that's okay, *if* you actually speak to Him with expectation. Healing through the Holy Spirit is very real, but it requires honest fellowship.

If you are not yet at the place where you can clearly hear His voice or sense His response, then speak to someone you trust.

When you are the one helping someone else recount

And if you're walking someone else through this process, understand the weight of what you're doing. Whether it's sexual abuse, mental abuse, or something else, guiding someone through their trauma is like drawing poison out of their body. You need to be careful because if you're not, that poison can enter you. As it's shared with you, give it to Christ. Let it pass through you, not stay in you. Don't dwell on it and don't revisit it in your mind. Forget it intentionally is how to protect your own heart.

Ask the person these probing questions:

- What happened?

- How did you feel?

- What else happened?

This part can be deeply painful, going through everything in detail. In the story of the woman caught in adultery, the people recounted the incident on her behalf, but she still had to be present. She had to stand there and listen without speaking.

Many people delay their restoration out of fear or a lack of trust. They hold back details, not knowing they are leaving behind what the Bible calls "little foxes." Every single detail must be brought out. You must be vulnerable, and in the right space. This process may bring tears, anger, or even numbness, but it cannot be skipped.

Step 3: Re-Evaluate the Incident

The wisdom of God is essential in this step, because it's not just what happened to you that caused the trauma, it's how you interpreted what happened. This is why whoever is walking with you in healing must be equipped to help you re-evaluate your story in light of God's truth. This is not about throwing around feel-good statements to pacify emotions. It's about bringing light into darkness. It's about helping someone see the situation through the eyes of truth.

Let's take sexual abuse of a young child as an example, since it is unfortunately very common. Many individuals won't even remember it until they hit a particular stage in life. But when they do, it often comes like a flood. After recounting the experience and there is no emotional response—no tears, no breaking—it may indicate a deeper issue. There should be a point of breaking. Most times, genuine healing begins at the point of brokenness.

For a little boy or girl who was abused, someone failed them. It was never their responsibility to protect themselves. A father failed. A mother failed. Perhaps it was a sibling, a teacher, or even a whole community that was silent when they should have spoken. Healing begins when the weight of blame is lifted off the child and laid where it rightfully belongs—on those who were meant to guard them and didn't.

Dealing with Guilt

It is important that you stay in God's presence with the right help until all your accusers are gone.

Jesus didn't release the woman caught in adultery until all her accusers had walked away. In your case, the accusers may not be physical people, it may be the condemning voices in your mind. But Jesus asks the same question: *"Where are those accusers of yours?"* And she responded, *"They're all gone."* That's when Jesus said, *"Neither do I condemn you."*

Jesus knew what was happening in that woman's case was unfair. If those Pharisees truly cared about justice, where was the man? Why was she the only one being dragged out and humiliated?

One of the strange side effects of trauma is guilt. Victims often carry the false sense that they somehow caused it. And once guilt enters, it begins to erode your faith. You begin to wonder if God is angry with you, or disappointed. But healing restores your faith. Like the woman, some people are able to quickly receive Jesus' words— *"Neither do I condemn you"* —and begin their restoration immediately. Others may take longer, and that's okay.

Trauma's Impact on Your Faith

Trauma doesn't just affect your emotions, it also impacts your faith. Victims often carry the false sense that they somehow caused it. And once guilt enters, it begins to erode your faith. It takes faith to accept that God is still pleased with you. For some, that alignment happens in a moment. For others, it takes weeks, even months. But the moment your heart comes into agreement with God, everything begins to shift.

In *Matthew 8*, Jesus marvelled at the centurion's faith, not because he had never seen faith before, but because the centurion believed without needing physical proof. Imagine going to a pastor and saying, *"I'm afraid to sleep without the lights on,"* and the pastor simply replies, *"You're free. Go home and sleep with the lights off."* It takes faith to obey that word.

Everything in the Kingdom operates by faith. The greater your faith, the quicker your restoration. The lesser your faith, the longer the journey. It's not that God is slow to move, it's that healing happens as you align with His pace.

Re-evaluating the incident means looking at it through new eyes—eyes informed by God's truth. It's a revolution of the mind, a rewiring of thoughts. Sometimes, the process is so delicate it's like undergoing surgery. And in some cases, the Holy Spirit may need to "put you to sleep" spiritually—not to ignore your pain, but to do deep work in your soul without the resistance of fear or misunderstanding.

Forgiveness of the Offender(s)

Forgiveness can be one of the most difficult steps for people walking through trauma. When you forgive a molester or someone who deeply hurt you, it may feel like you're letting them off the hook, but in reality, you're setting yourself free. Forgiveness isn't about excusing what they did. It's about freeing yourself from their grip.

When you forgive, you are not saying they're innocent. You are saying, *"I'm no longer holding this in my hands. I'm placing it in God's."* In places where the rule of law exists, people are judged not by individuals, but by the legal system. In the same way, God is the ultimate lawkeeper. When you forgive, you let Him judge the matter.

Even if the abuse happened years ago, it can still be reported. But you need to forgive first. Many people have been traumatized by Church experiences—leaders, members, and environments that didn't reflect Christ. That's why some find it hard to trust or stay rooted in a Church. They wonder, *"Is this joy I feel even real? Or is it just pretense again?"* Re-evaluation helps you find perspective. And with perspective, comes the grace to forgive.

Step 4: Reformation of Your Nature

Reformation means beginning the journey back to what your life was meant to be. It's a long road, but the earlier you start, the better. Trauma affects more than emotions. It distorts your understanding of love, relationships, purpose, and even your own body. Even after healing, you may need to relearn healthy ways of living.

After abuse, people often develop dysfunctional patterns, especially in marriage, sex, parenting, and communication. Reformation comes through the Word of God, the help of the Holy Spirit, wise counsel, and the discipline of mentorship. A structured life will teach you how things ought to be.

Trauma may have shaped how you relate to food, for example, maybe you overeat when stressed or under-eat to feel in control. It's like someone who had an accident that requires physiotherapy to learn how to walk properly again.

A man cannot truly be a godly husband if he's still operating from trauma, even if he's been "healed." He must learn what a husband is supposed to be. He must see Christ as the model. Just like Jesus is the husband and the Church is His bride, men must learn to be coverings, not critics. The same applies to a wife who may have been traumatized. A woman traumatized by bullying may walk around expecting to be attacked, always ready to fight, even when there's no danger and may struggle with submitting to her husband.

Reformation means realizing that not everyone is out to get you. Yes, some people are wicked, but many are simply weak. You must learn self-control and wisdom in how you respond to both. Freedom comes when your responses are no longer driven by past wounds.

If you've experienced rejection, you need to rewire your thinking. Not everyone will accept you, and that's okay. It doesn't always mean you're being rejected, it means people have the right to choose. Like the process of job hunting, you don't stop applying just because one place says no. You keep going until you find the right fit.

Life is good on the other side of healing. But you must begin the reformation process, and keep walking it for the rest of your life. That's what Jesus meant when He told the woman, *"Go and sin no more."* (John 8:11) That statement implies she now had to learn what sin actually was. If she knew how not to sin, she likely wouldn't have fallen into it in the first place.

She may have needed to read Scripture, listen to Jesus' teachings, or follow someone like Mary Magdalene or the women who supported Jesus. She may have needed a mentor, like Ruth had Naomi. You need someone who can show you what a healed life looks like.

The Process of Reformation

Discipline Your Mind

One of the most important aspects of reformation is learning to discipline your mind. It begins with understanding the damage certain thoughts can cause to the soul. When Jesus told the woman, *"Go and sin no more,"* that directive wasn't just about behaviour—it involved a transformation of the mind.

Books like *The Power of Positive Thinking* by Norman Vincent Peale and *The Disciplined Life* by Calvin Miller have been a blessing in this regard. They offer practical principles that can renew the mind and redirect your thoughts in alignment with God's Word.

If you haven't yet learned how to think positively, your mind cannot function as it should. Look at Jesus as our example—when they told Him Lazarus was dead, He said, *"He is sleeping."* Why? Because He didn't want to confess death. That is a sign of a disciplined mind. Anything I don't want, I don't dwell on. I don't say, *"I am weak,"* I say, *"I am strong."* That's the discipline of the mind.

Many people joke carelessly with negative words. They say things like, *"I'm dead,"* and then they walk around carrying the weight of those words. But when they come into Church, we revive them through the power of God's Word.

I strongly encourage you to read those books I mentioned, especially *The Disciplined Life*. The principles there apply to every area of life. The Bible summarizes it best in Philippians 4:6-9: *"Be anxious for nothing, but in everything by prayer and supplication, with thanksgiving, let your requests be made known to God; and the peace of God, which surpasses all understanding, will guard your hearts and minds through Christ Jesus."*

A healthy, disciplined mind is guarded by peace.

Discipline Your Emotions

A healthy emotional life is one that can receive love, process love, and give love—just like a healthy heart receives blood, processes it, and sends it out again. *"In this is love, not that we loved God, but that He loved us and sent His Son… Beloved, if God so loved us, we also ought to love one another."* (1 John 4:10-11)

Disciplined emotions can forgive, give and serve. But when emotions are undisciplined, they harbour offence, prolong sadness, and live in cycles of discouragement and disappointment.

The evidence of a disciplined emotional life is confidence in love and confidence with those around you. As it says in 1 John 4:17-18, perfect love drives out fear. Disciplined emotions don't retaliate. You can be hurt, but you don't hit back. It's about keeping a proper heart.

Discipline Your Will

A disciplined will is marked by self-control and submission. Pride is a sign of an undisciplined will. But when your will is disciplined, your "yes" is yes and your "no" is no. You are able to submit to the Word of God, to the voice of the Holy Spirit, and to the human authority He has placed over your life.

In 1 John 4:1–6, we are instructed not to believe every spirit, but to test the spirits. That's what a disciplined spirit does—it discerns. Just as your nose smells food before you eat, your spirit must test what's being presented to it. Discernment is part of a disciplined life.

How Do You Know You Are Free and Stay Free?

You know that trauma has been dealt with when you can remember the incident, but you no longer feel emotionally tied to it. Deliverance doesn't always mean forgetting; it means you can remember without pain.

Counselling plays a big role in this. And when I say "counsellor," I'm not necessarily referring to someone with a degree, but to someone with God-given grace to walk others through healing.

Sometimes deliverance comes through counselling. Other times it comes through the laying on of hands or other spiritual encounters. The key is discernment—knowing whether the root issue is emotional, mental, or spiritual. Kenneth E. Hagin once shared how trauma led him to violent tendencies. But once he was taught the right way to process those feelings, healing came.

Our role in renewing the soul is to extract Kingdom principles from Scripture that govern the mind, emotions, and will. That's why I wrote *A Disciplined Life*—to show how the soul can return to the way God intended it to function.

Learning how emotions work is part of spiritual maturity. I remember recently watching the funeral of a soldier of Christ in Nigeria—it moved me to tears. And I thought of how Jesus wept when He saw Mary crying (John 11:35). As believers, we must learn how to feel and process our emotions, how to love and how to be angry without sinning. Expressing anger could be as simple as saying, *"I'm not happy with what you did. Please don't do it again."* That's healthy.

A healthy soul doesn't keep records of wrongs. Constantly rehearsing past offences only builds tension. *"Love covers a multitude of sins."* (1 Peter 4:8) Let the Word of God minister to your soul during your devotional time. Ask, *"What needs to be corrected in me?"*

7
Victory in the Mind

THE BATTLEFIELD OF THOUGHTS

From the Word of God, we understand that a person becomes what they continually think. The course of your life will always follow the pattern of your thoughts. Many times, people fall into temptation, settle into mediocrity, or shrink in fear and failure, not because they lack potential, but because they've accepted the lies the enemy whispered into their minds.

Attacks on Your Thoughts

The enemy has no business with the present. He is always targeting your past and your future. That's where the mind wars begin. In the spiritual realm, there is no "now." There is only what has been and what is to come. And the enemy knows that if he can distort your view of where you've been, or corrupt your expectation of what's ahead, he can trap you where you are.

Even in the natural realm, this principle holds. When U.S. President Donald Trump inaugurated the Space Force, another branch of the US military alongside the Army and Air Force it wasn't because there was a war in space. It was because they knew the next war would be fought *there*. Some people are still stuck reliving yesterday's pain, but others are already preparing for battles of tomorrow.

Which Battle Are You Fighting?

My question to you is: **what battle are you fighting now?** Are you still waging war over old wounds? Or are you preparing for the future, laying hold of what's ahead?

Victory in the mind requires time travel. That's why trauma is so dangerous. It keeps you stuck in the past, forcing you to relive battles that were never resolved. But when God steps in, He goes *back* to win those wars on your behalf. And once that's settled, He gives you grace to step *forward* and begin preparing for the future.

Some of us today are walking in peace we didn't even fight for. Others fought and won those battles in the place of prayer. That's why prayer is not just for emergencies but also for preparation. You don't just pray because there's trouble; you pray always so that when trouble comes, it finds you already covered.

The Bible says, *"Woe to those who are at ease in Zion."* (Amos 6:1) You don't rest because you had one victory. You fight until every territory is taken. You don't say, *"Let us eat and drink, for tomorrow we die."* (1 Corinthians 15:32) That's the language of defeat.

We are not of those who give up. We are of those who rise up, who fight forward, and who win perpetually.

And I pray for you, in the name of Jesus, that you will win in your mind. That your thoughts will be filled with light. That every word you hear will be filtered through the truth of God's Word.

Distinguishing Thoughts

A few major questions you must ask yourself today is this:

Do you know what your thoughts sound like? Do you know which ones are yours? Which ones are from the enemy? Which ones are from God?

God's thoughts are always filled with life while the devil's thoughts are always filled with fear, accusation, and confusion. Your thoughts, by default, are analytical—they weigh and consider. But many people don't know how to discern between the three. So when the devil whispers, *"You're not enough,"* or *"It's going to fail,"* they say, *"Well, my mind is telling me..."* That wasn't your mind. That was the enemy.

If a thought aligns with the Word of God and produces faith, it's from God. If it produces fear, shame, guilt, or rebellion, it's from the enemy. Don't entertain it—*cast it down* in the name of Jesus.

2 Corinthians 10:5 commands us to *"cast down arguments and every high thing that exalts itself against the knowledge of God."* That means anything that challenges the truth of God's Word must be torn down immediately, before it takes root.

THE MIND IS THE ENGINE ROOM OF LIFE

Whoever supplies the raw materials for your thinking ultimately steers the direction of your life.

The greatest attack on a person is not on their body, it's on their mind. A person may be physically limited, yet still thrive and make impact. But if the mind is broken, the whole person is paralyzed. That's because your mind is the engine room of your life. It governs how you see the past, how you process the present, and how you pursue the future.

Tell a child over and over that they will fail and unless God intervenes, they'll grow up and fulfill that expectation. Why? Because thoughts shape reality.

Here are a few things you must understand about the mind:

It's not what happens to you, it's how you interpret it.

Two people can go through the exact same thing. One becomes bitter, the other becomes better. The difference is how they processed it. That's why the mind is so powerful. It doesn't just store memory, it tells you what that memory *means*.

The mind is the only part of you that tries to explain itself.

Your mind will go through something, and then try to tell you what happened. And that's where the enemy loves to operate. He doesn't just bring hardship, he offers commentary and gives you an interpretation.

The Example of Job

Look at Job. The devil asked for permission to test him. God allowed it, not because He wanted to harm Job, but because He trusted him. Imagine if Job had known that, he would've rejoiced, saying, *"Wow, God believes in me. I'm honoured."*

But the enemy didn't just bring affliction, he also brought misinterpretation. He made Job believe that God was against him, when in reality, it was God who preserved his life and set the boundary saying, *"You can go this far, and no more."* (Job 1:12; 2:6)

Beloved, this is why we must win the battle in the mind. Victory doesn't start with what's around you. It starts with what's within you. And today, by the grace of God, may your mind be renewed and aligned with truth, in Jesus' name.

WORDS YOU HEAR DETERMINE WHAT YOU SEE

The mind is built to receive, interpret, and process information. And just as the physical world runs on words, so does the mind. What you continually hear will eventually shape what you begin to see.

Before Goliath ever lifted a weapon against Israel, he launched a war of words. Morning and evening for 40 days, he stood before God's people, taunting them, threatening them, painting pictures of their destruction with his words. Why didn't he just attack? Because he knew that if he could win the battle in their minds, he wouldn't have to fight them physically.

That's how the devil works. He sends words—through dreams, through imaginations, through fears—long before anything ever manifests.

He shows you a vision of an accident. You wake up unsettled, shaken. And if you're not careful, that fear begins to open a door.

He shows you a dream where your marriage is falling apart, so you begin to overanalyze, to react in fear, to question everything. Not realizing that it was never about the dream itself, it was about planting a seed of destruction through fear.

He shows you exam results in red ink. You see yourself failing, again and again. And if you're not spiritually alert, you begin to prepare for failure instead of success.

But I decree over you that every demonic picture, every satanic imagination, every lie whispered into your mind is uprooted now, in Jesus name!

What You See Is What You Become

You see, no one can go beyond the revelation they've received. Humanity was able to go to the moon not because of strength, but because of insight and revelation. And the same principle applies in the spirit. Nobody rises into a destiny they have not first seen with the eyes of their mind.

Proverbs 23:7 says, *"For as he thinks in his heart, so is he."* As she thinks in her heart, so is she. As a nation thinks in its heart, so it becomes. That's why the real warfare begins in the mind.

You can never be defeated unless you've already lost the battle in your thinking. Even in physical war, they don't start with bullets, they start with information. That's why propaganda is always the first strike.

During the Cold War, South Korea set up loudspeakers pointed toward the North, broadcasting messages about freedom, prosperity, and life outside the regime. They weren't firing missiles but were firing truth. They even dropped flyers from the sky, showing what life looked like on the other side. Why? Because they knew that if the people ever *saw* the truth, it would only be a matter of time before they walked into freedom.

That's what happens when we come into the presence of God. He holds up a mirror, not just to show us who we've been, but who He says we are. And once you see it, by His grace, you begin to become it.

RENEWING YOUR MIND

Romans 12:2 says, *"Do not be conformed to this world, but be transformed by the renewing of your mind."* We all know how to cleanse our bodies but do you know how to wash your mind? Some of us shower every morning, moisturize, and get dressed in our best yet we walk around with minds that haven't been renewed in months. We bathe our bodies in soap but leave our minds soaked in filth.

When you find yourself constantly offended, always assuming the worst and drowning in suspicion and negativity, know that it's not the people around you, it's your mind crying out for renewal.

And how is the mind renewed? By soaking and cleansing it with the Word of God.

Be vigilant over your mind. Don't let just anything grow there. Fill your environment with worship, pray in the Spirit, meditate on the Word, and surround yourself with people that speak life. Because at the end of the day, your life will reflect the condition of your mind.

Speak the Truth

A victorious mind is not built casually. Just like you don't get a strong body by accident, you don't get a strong mind by chance. It is developed intentionally through the quality of thoughts you entertain and the words you allow to take root.

Think about the placebo effect. People receive sugar pills, yet recover—simply because they *believe* they're getting real medicine. Their mind starts to heal the body based on a belief. That's the power of the mind. *The mind creates the moment.* If you believe you're rising, your whole being will start to align with that direction.

And if that's what a natural mind can do—imagine what a *renewed* mind can do.

Job 6:25 says, *"How forcible are right words!"* There's weight to the words you speak—especially in the midst of adversity. Words declared in peacetime carry one kind of weight, but words spoken in war? They are spiritual weapons.

Sadly, many people drop the sword right when the battle begins. They forget everything they've ever believed. That's like a child letting go of their father's hand in a thunderstorm. That's not the time to let go, that's the time to hold on tighter.

I pray that where fear made you let go, faith will help you grab hold again. May your grip on God and His Word be strengthened, in Jesus' name.

Avoid Anxiety and Worry

Let me share a truth that will liberate you: *What will happen, will happen.*

Think back to the things you once worried about. Some happened and some didn't. But one thing is certain: you're still here. Still breathing and still standing.

Worry is both unnecessary and destructive. It's like a person spinning in circles until they collapse from dizziness. That's what anxiety does to your mind—it keeps you busy doing nothing and gets you tired over things you cannot change.

If you are worried about graduation, focus on passing your current classes. Instead of worrying about turning 30 and not having figuring things out, celebrate your growth and embrace the process. Purpose is not a destination—it unfolds as you move.

Worry never makes sense. And if you knew how much weight it puts on your soul, you'd drop it immediately.

Esther said, *"If I perish, I perish."* (Esther 4:16) That wasn't carelessness—it was courage. She did her part, and she left the rest in God's hands.

8

How To Help the Traumatized

IDENTIFY THAT THEY ARE TRAUMATIZED

The first step in helping a traumatized person is to quickly and prayerfully discern whether or not they are indeed traumatized. This is not just for their benefit, it's also essential for your own well-being and safety.

When Saul first tried to kill David, David didn't run. He stayed and continued to serve him faithfully. But when it happened again, something clicked: *"This man is unstable. Give him space. Serve him from afar."* David realized that staying too close would put his life at risk.

Eventually, David stepped away from his role as Saul's armour-bearer, but he didn't stop honouring the king. He just knew he had to reposition himself. As Christians, we are not called to remain in environments that are harmful, where someone's brokenness turns us into a target. The Lord is not only our Shepherd, He is also our wisdom. And it's with that wisdom that we must know when to create space.

A traumatized person is often unstable, unpredictable. That's why it's so important to recognize it early. If you fail to discern it, your good intentions could lead to unnecessary harm, both for them and for you.

GIVE THEM WHAT THEY ARE LACKING

Once you've identified that someone is dealing with trauma, the next step is to give them what they're truly lacking—not what they're saying, but what their soul is silently crying out for.

Too often, people respond by talking too much or trying to fix the situation through conversation alone. Some even place burdens on the traumatized person, expecting emotional or practical support from someone who's barely holding on. But in 1 Kings 19, the angel of the Lord responded to Elijah differently, with wisdom and discernment.

Elijah was venting, saying he wanted to die. But the angel didn't react to the words; he looked past them. Trauma distorts communication. People rarely mean exactly what they say when they're hurting. *"I hate this family,"* might actually mean, *"I love you all deeply, and I'm heartbroken." "I'm leaving and never coming back,"* might really mean, *"I need space, but I'm still hoping you'll wait for me."*

The angel responded not with correction, but with compassion. He placed a cake baked on coals by Elijah's head—something warm, comforting, and inviting. Not a lecture. Not even fish and bread, which God had provided in other moments. But cake. Because sometimes, what a person needs most is something sweet to remind them that life is still good.

When you're helping someone who is traumatized, focus less on fixing them and more on caring for them. A small, thoughtful act—like their favourite snack, a quiet shopping trip, or simply sitting with them—can speak louder than any sermon. Pray before you do it. Ask God for peace and grace to surround that time. You might be surprised how someone can go from weeping to laughing in the space of a few minutes.

There's a story of a couple in marriage counselling. The wife said, *"In my entire marriage, I've never been happy. Not one day."* Her husband was shocked. *"Not one day? What about the vacations, the gifts, the laughter?"* The counsellor calmly responded, *"Sir, she's not talking about the past. She's telling you how she feels right now."*

This is how we must approach those who are hurting. Don't dissect their words, discern their needs. Elijah wasn't just tired, he was spiritually drained, emotionally weary, and completely alone. So the angel met him where he was. No long speech. Just food, water and rest. And even after all that, the angel came back again. *"Arise and eat again."* The angel returned with more sustenance, because healing takes time. And note that he didn't linger. He served, then stepped back.

When helping a traumatized person, love them, but protect your own soul in the process. You can show care without overexposing yourself. Their pain, if you're not careful, can become your own. And later, even when they've healed, you might struggle to connect again because you've been wounded by what they said or did in survival mode.

You must be wise. Serve them gently and offer them what feeds their soul. And if you can afford it, whether it's a gift, a moment of peace, or just your presence, give it freely. But don't expect it to fix everything at once.

Healing rarely happens in one encounter. Sometimes, you'll need to come back again, just like the angel did.

GIVE THEM SPACE

One of the quickest ways to become drained is to stay with a traumatized person unprotected. You may think you're helping them, but in the process, you're also depleting your own strength. There is such a thing as tough love, but it's still love. Don't spend hours on the phone listening to all the toxic things a traumatized person shares. It's not sustainable. You must know when to lovingly draw the line.

In a relationship, don't be the one carrying your partner's trauma if you can help it. If you want your relationship to last, bring someone else in to help. It's like the advice not to teach your partner how to drive, because you might not remain their partner afterwards. You may be wise, gifted, and even a great counsellor, but when you assume the role of the healer, you put the health of the relationship at risk.

The role of a doctor during childbirth is a good example. The woman doesn't go home with the doctor, she goes home with her husband. Yet the doctor is the one who carries the weight of what was seen and experienced. The same event is lived very differently by each person involved. Likewise, the angel ministering to Elijah eventually passed him on. Notice that the angel didn't stay and argue or go back and forth with him. There is a higher power, a higher authority, that can speak to a traumatized person in a way that they will listen and respond. The angel did what was necessary, and then handed Elijah over to God.

Work with the Traumatized with Love

When working with individuals who have experienced trauma, it is crucial to approach them with empathy, patience, and understanding. But also, remember that caregivers and those who walk closely with the traumatized need support too. You must care for yourself while caring for others.

Here are a few key principles to keep in mind:

Recognize the Impact of Trauma
Traumatic experiences can deeply affect a person's behaviour, emotions, and overall well-being. Don't be surprised when their responses don't match your expectations. They're often navigating life through a distorted lens of fear and survival.

Practice Patience and Empathy
Be patient and empathetic in your interactions. Don't take their behaviour personally. Instead, strive to create an atmosphere that feels safe and supportive.

Provide a Listening Ear
Sometimes what a traumatized person needs most is someone who will simply listen. Not someone to fix them or correct them—but someone who will sit with them, validate their pain, and give them space to express what they're carrying at their own pace.

Maintain Boundaries
It's important to be supportive, but not at the cost of your own health. You are not Jesus. Establish and protect healthy boundaries so you don't take on more than you can handle emotionally or spiritually.

Seek Support for Yourself

Caring for others, especially those who are deeply wounded, can be exhausting. You must make sure your own tank is not running on empty. Find safe people to talk to, fill your love tank regularly and seek help when you need it.

ENCOURAGE PROFESSIONAL HELP

Encourage the traumatized to seek professional help—from trained therapists or counsellors who specialize in trauma recovery. Recognize the limits of your role and the importance of expert guidance. Sometimes the best thing you can do for someone is point them to a resource that can walk with them at a deeper level.

"Blessed are the poor in spirit, for theirs is the kingdom of heaven." (Matthew 5:3) This reminds us that those who are broken and burdened are especially close to the heart of God. As we work with the traumatized, let us reflect God's compassion and love, while leaning on His wisdom and strength to navigate these often challenging situations.

A traumatized person is primarily focused on avoiding pain. That's the lens through which they see the world. Their decisions are built around minimizing threat, not necessarily around doing what is right or reasonable. They are constantly asking themselves, *"How can I avoid pain right now?"* And sometimes, that will lead them to lie, steal, gossip, or shut people out, not because they're evil, but because they're desperate.

Knowing this helps you not to take it personally. It helps you love wisely. Because if you're not careful, you can get wounded trying to help someone who hasn't yet realized they're bleeding.

Extend Grace to People

In the Church, we often encounter people who have gone through deep, unspeakable trauma. You smile at them and they don't smile back. You greet them and they walk away or respond coldly. Maybe they overreact to something small, and you're left wondering, *What's wrong with this person?* The temptation is to say, *"Good riddance to bad rubbish,"* and keep your distance. But the truth is, the Church is not a museum of perfect people, it's a hospital for the wounded.

If you truly knew the story of the person sitting next to you, you might be far more gracious. I recently met someone whose story deeply moved me. This person had been locked away without food, ran away from home at a young age, and was taken in by a complete stranger. They practically had to raise themselves, while both parents were still alive. You'd never guess that by looking at them. People's pain is often hidden behind well-dressed appearances, but the scars are real.

As members of the body of Christ, we must learn to extend grace, especially when it hasn't been earned. People don't owe you their testimony just because you attend the same Church. You're not their pastor. But even when someone walks past you without greeting, or storms away in anger, choose to respond with understanding. You don't know the road they've walked.

Imagine crossing paths with Elijah on his way to the mountain. In his brokenness, he might not even acknowledge you. He might mistake you for the enemy and say, *"You're one of them. Leave me alone."* In that moment, extend grace. Respect their space. Love them from a distance. It takes maturity to see people through the lens of compassion instead of offence.

DEALING WITH SUICIDAL PEOPLE

Pastoring, parenting, mentoring, all require the same delicate balance of being present without being overbearing. Especially when dealing with someone who is suicidal, your approach in each of these relationship dynamics matters.

In Elijah's case, he said, *"It is enough; now, Lord, take my life."* But he had no clear plan to end it. His words were heavy, yes—but they were also a cry for relief, a cry for someone to notice. And God noticed. The angel brought him food. He didn't rebuke Elijah. He didn't rush into panic. He softly addressed the need behind the outburst.

Sometimes, suicidal thoughts are more about wanting the pain to stop than wanting life to end. In those moments, listen. Don't overreact or make them feel trapped. Let them speak freely and provide comfort without pressure.

But there's a difference between ideation and intention.

If someone is actively suicidal, with both the will and the means to carry out their plan, then immediate action is necessary. In such cases:

- Stay close and monitor them closely

- Remove anything that could be used for self-harm

- Seek professional help and notify trusted support systems immediately

Remember, this is just the beginning of the conversation. Dealing with mental health issues and suicidal thoughts requires a comprehensive approach, including professional help, community support, and a loving, non-judgmental environment.

Epilogue

If you've made it to this point, I want to commend you—not just for finishing a book, but for confronting what many spend a lifetime avoiding. If you allowed the Holy Spirit to move through them, something within you has already begun to shift.

You now understand that trauma isn't always obvious. It hides in how you respond to love, correction, silence, or truth. It lives in the patterns you've normalized and the behaviours you've excused. But now, you have language for what you've lived through. You've seen it clearly. And you've been equipped to do something about it.

You've also learned that trauma isn't always random. Yes, some of it came through the wickedness of others. But some of it—though painful—was allowed by God as part of your formation. The cross you carry isn't a sign that you're cursed. It's often proof that you're being prepared. And when God permits pain, He always supplies grace to endure it and purpose beyond it.

But identifying the source of your trauma is only the beginning. Deliverance is not the finish line—it's the doorway. The goal is not just to be set free, but to remain free. And that requires more than a breakthrough moment. It requires the reformation of your entire being. Your mind must be renewed. Your emotions must be stabilized. Your will must be disciplined. Without that reformation, freedom won't last—you'll eventually drift back to the very place God brought you out of.

Lasting freedom comes through intentional living. Now that you've come this far, you must guard what you've gained. Don't allow old thoughts, emotional habits, or trauma-driven responses to convince you that nothing has changed. You have tools now. You have insight. You have discernment. And most importantly, you have access to the One who restores all things. But the decision to remain free? That belongs to you. God won't force you to walk in healing—you must choose it, every day.

So when the triggers come, remember what you've learned. When the urge to isolate creeps in, remind yourself: withdrawal is not healing. When the voice of accusation whispers again, respond with truth. Don't forget what the Lord has already revealed to you.

You are no longer just the one who endured pain—you are the one who overcame it. That is your new identity. You are not what they did to you. You are not who you were when the trauma occurred. You are now healed, restored, and whole.

"You shall be called by a new name, Which the mouth of the Lord will name. You shall also be a crown of glory in the hand of the Lord, And a royal diadem in the hand of your God. You shall no longer be termed Forsaken, Nor shall your land any more be termed Desolate; But you shall be called Hephzibah, and your land Beulah; For the Lord delights in you." (Isaiah 62:2–4)

Be bold in this new identity and understand that you do not owe anyone an apology for choosing to heal. You don't need to explain why you're no longer available for trauma-bonded relationships. You don't need permission to become the version of yourself that pain tried to bury.

So I leave you with this charge: don't drift back into old routines. Instead, build new thought patterns rooted in truth. Immerse yourself daily in the Word of God. Surround yourself with people who speak life. Seek accountability when needed, and stay planted in community. Above all, remain committed to the ongoing process of wholeness.

Contact the Author

I know without a doubt that this book has been a blessing to you. I am looking forward to hearing your testimony.

You can stay connected with me through the following platforms:

Instagram: e.adewusi | **Youtube:** Emmanuel Adewusi
Website: emmanueladewusi.org

Support the Author

Review the Book

A Sinner's Prayer

Dear Heavenly Father,

I come to You in the Name of Jesus Christ.

You said in Your Word, "Whosoever shall call upon the name of the Lord shall be saved." (Romans 10:13) I am calling on Your Name, so I know You have saved me now.

You also said that "if you confess with your mouth the Lord Jesus and believe in your heart that God has raised Him from the dead, you will be saved. For with the heart one believes unto righteousness, and with the mouth, confession is made unto salvation." (Romans 10:9-10) I believe in my heart Jesus Christ is the Son of God. I believe that He was raised from the dead for my justification, and I confess Him now as my Lord and Savior.

Thank you, Lord, because now, I am saved!

Thank You, Lord, because I know you have heard my prayer. Thank You, Lord, because I am now born again.

Signed _____

Date _____

About the Author

Apostle Emmanuel Adewusi is the Founding and Lead Pastor of Cornerstone Christian Church of God.

Called into ministry with the mandate to "bring restoration and transformation to all by teaching, preaching, and demonstrating the Gospel of Jesus Christ," he is passionate about seeing lives restored and transformed as God intended from the beginning of creation. He has a zeal for the full counsel of the Word of God, fellowship with the Holy Spirit, and being under spiritual authority.

He authored the books *"Now That You Are Born Again, What Next?"*, *"The Blessings of Being Under Spiritual Authority,"* *"A Disciplined Life,"* *"The Enlightened Believer,"* *"The Skilled Sower,"* and other impactful titles. He has also released an album titled *"Divine Encounter"* and many more on the way.

Emmanuel Adewusi is joyfully married to his wife, Ibukun Adewusi, and together, they are building a thriving Christ-centered family.

www.ingramcontent.com/pod-product-compliance
Lightning Source LLC
Chambersburg PA
CBHW050250010526
44107CB00003B/257